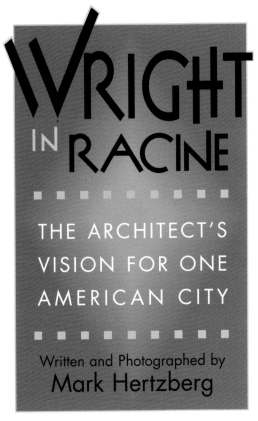

WRIGHT IN RACINE

THE ARCHITECT'S VISION FOR ONE AMERICAN CITY

Written and Photographed by

Mark Hertzberg

Introduction by Edgar Tafel

SAN FRANCISCO

Published by Pomegranate Communications, Inc.
Box 808022, Petaluma CA 94975
800 227 1428; www.pomegranate.com

Pomegranate Europe Ltd.
Unit 1, Heathcote Business Centre
Hurlbutt Road, Warwick
Warwickshire CV34 6TD, U.K.
[+44] 0 1926 430111

Library of Congress Cataloging-in-Publication Data

Hertzberg, Mark.
    Wright in Racine : the architect's vision for one American city / Mark Hertzberg.
        p. cm.
    ISBN 0-7649-2890-2 (alk. paper)
     1. Wright, Frank Lloyd, 1867–1959. 2. Architecture—Wisconsin—Racine—20th century.
 3. Racine (Wis.)—Buildings, structures, etc. I. Wright, Frank Lloyd, 1867–1959. II. Title.

NA737.W7H465 2004
720'.92—dc22

                                                2004044616

Pomegranate Catalog No. A754

Design by Shannon Lemme

Printed in Korea

13 12 11 10 09 08 07 06 05   10 9 8 7 6 5 4 3 2

This book is fondly dedicated to the memories of Elsie Steiner, my grandmother; Joan Naumberg Hertzberg, my aunt; and "Miz M.," Ellen Mosey, the director of the Lake Forest College of Public Information, who gave me my first paid photo assignments, and was a friend, as well as a mentor.

Wingspread is magnificent during the peak of Wisconsin's fall colors.

■ ■ ■

Preface 6
Acknowledgments 9
Introduction by Edgar Tafel 11

Chapter 1 ■ Private Homes 13
       Cecil Corwin and Frank Lloyd Wright—The Miles House (1901)   *13*
       The Hardy House (1905)   *16*
       Wingspread (1937)   *25*
       The Roy Petersen House (1941)   *40*
       The Keland House (1954)   *41*

Chapter 2 ■ Public Buildings 51
       SC Johnson Administration Building (1936)   *51*
       Airport Lounge/Café Project (1941)   *65*
       SC Johnson Research Tower (1944)   *67*
       YWCA (1949, 1950)   *75*

Chapter 3 ■ Affordable Housing 79
       The Monolith Homes (1919)   *79*
       The Johnson Homes (1948)   *81*

Appendixes
       A Tower Letter from Wright to H. F. Johnson Jr. 82
       B Wright in Racine Project List 83
       C Racine Work of Former Apprentices and Associates 84
       D Resources 85
Endnotes 86
Bibliography 93

Frank Lloyd Wright's architectural legacy is indisputable. His revolutionary designs redefined the spaces in which we live and work, although many people are unaware just how much his ideas have influenced our homes and businesses.

Wright was concerned about the space around his buildings as much as he was concerned about the buildings themselves: "The good building is not one that hurts the landscape, but one which makes the landscape more beautiful than it was before the building was built."[1] Wright was a genius who was often vilified when he was alive, because his personal life offended so many people. His buildings were frequently over budget, and they sometimes leaked, but they had a profound effect on people. He seemed to thrive on controversy, whether it was about his personal views, or about his often startling and revolutionary designs. He made it sound like a simple choice—"Very early in my life, I had to choose between honest arrogance and hypocritical humility, and I chose honest arrogance."[2]

Wright's legacy has grown immeasurably since his death in 1959. People come from around the world to see his buildings; about 4,000 people take the weekly architectural tour of the SC Johnson Administration Building every year. More books have been written about Wright than about any other architect, and gift shops sell every kind of Wright souvenir imaginable.[3]

The city of Racine, Wisconsin, encompasses the breadth of Wright's career with an unusually wide variety of work from almost every significant stage of the architect's career after 1900. Racine is nestled on the Lake Michigan shoreline between Chicago, where Wright began his career in 1887, and Milwaukee. It was founded in 1834, and became a city of robust industry.

Racine attracted a variety of ambitious, inventive people, and it celebrates its heritage as the "invention city."[4] Case Company threshers and farm tractors, Horlick's Malted Milk, and Golden Books all originated in Racine.[5] Chester Beach invented the fractional horsepower universal motor in Racine; it was adapted to many household uses, including the Hamilton Beach, Osterizer, and Waring blenders. Albert Dremel invented the first gasoline-powered lawn mower in Racine, and John Hammes invented the In-Sink-Erator, the first garbage disposal machine. Handheld hair dryers, the first portable vacuum cleaner, and even a lollipop-making machine were invented in Racine.

In 1886, Samuel Curtis Johnson founded the S. C. Johnson Company in this city that nurtured such creativity when he bought the Racine Hardware Company's parquet flooring business.[6] Johnson's customers wanted to know how to preserve their floors, and his research and experiments led to the development of Johnson's Prepared Paste Wax.

Soon, each new floor was shipped with cans of the wax. By 1917, the demand for parquet flooring had diminished, but the demand for Johnson's Wax and related finishing products continued to grow, so the company stopped selling flooring.

Wright's first commission in Racine was in 1901, when he drew several proposals for the remodel of Herbert and Flora Miles' home. His designs show strong early Prairie elements added to an existing, small house.[7] He received his first commission to build, rather than remodel, a home in Racine in 1905, when he built a Prairie house for attorney Thomas P. Hardy into a bluff that faces Lake Michigan. The location embodies Wright's principle of organic architecture, intertwining the house and the land, rather than simply placing it on top of the lot, as was the custom.

Hardy commissioned the Monolith Homes, a community housing project, in 1919, when Wright was in Tokyo working on the Imperial Hotel. The designs were actually rendered by draftsman Rudolph Schindler, in Wright's name, and Wright received a patent for the concrete engineering he proposed for the project.[8]

Wright returned to Racine in 1936, fifty years after Samuel Curtis Johnson founded his company, to design the landmark SC Johnson Administration Building. The building helped to define the company as much as it helped to redefine Wright's career when it opened in 1939. H. F. Johnson Jr. would become not only one of Frank Lloyd Wright's most famous clients, but also one of Wright's favorite clients.[9]

A year after the Administration Building commission, Johnson hired Wright to design Wingspread, a zoned house that is considered Wright's last and largest Prairie home.

In 1941 Wright suggested an unbuilt Usonian home design (the Carlson house, 1939) to Roy Petersen, a Racine client who worked for Johnson.[10] Later that year, at Johnson's request, Wright drew floor plans for another unbuilt proposal, to turn an existing home into a combination pilots' lounge and café at the Racine airport.

Three years later, Wright designed the SC Johnson Research Tower. It was the first time that he was able to implement the tap-root tower scheme he had first proposed in 1929 for St. Marks-in-the-Bouwerie, a twenty-three-story apartment building project in New York City.[11]

In 1949, Johnson hired Wright yet again, to design the new Racine YWCA building. Wright submitted plans for a dramatic building with a swimming pool under a glass roof. Board members questioned the costs and feasibility of his proposal. Wright withdrew from the project because the Board also consulted two other architects.[12]

Wright designed a home for Karen [Johnson's daughter] and Willard Keland in 1954, five years before he died. The floor plan is similar to those in his Usonian homes, although it is larger than most of them.

Wright was important to Racine, and Racine was important to Wright, particularly because of the SC Johnson Administration Building. Edgar Tafel, one of the first apprentices in the Taliesin Fellowship, the architectural school Wright started in 1932 when he had little work and was hungry for new sources of income, notes that "Racine gave him the opportunity. If he had a career, he would not have started the school."[13]

Wright has left a legacy in Racine. "Wright is a part of what we [SC Johnson] are and what we represent," says Samuel C. "Sam" Johnson, H. F. Johnson Jr.'s son and chairman emeritus of SC Johnson.[14] The cars with license plates from around the country that slow down near the Hardy house and fill the nearby Johnson parking lot on tour day underscore that legacy.

It was a challenge to continue working full time while researching and writing this book to meet the publisher's ambitious four-month deadline. Many people gave me their support and generously shared their time and knowledge to help make this book possible. I of course owe special thanks to my family: to my wife, Cindy, and to our sons, Adam and Aaron, for their love and encouragement; to my in-laws, Curtis and Virginia Westfall, for giving me a "quiet zone" when we visited them; and to my brother, Michael Lee Hertzberg, and his family, Alexa Stellings and Niki Stellings-Hertzberg, for a birthday gift that evolved into this book. Fenway, our golden retriever, faithfully kept me company many long nights as I worked on the book.

I am particularly indebted to H. F. Johnson Jr.'s son and daughter, Sam Johnson and Karen Johnson Boyd. Sam encouraged me to write the story of Wright's work in Racine, the city he loves so well, on a day when I mentioned the idea of a book, never dreaming that it would be written within seven months. He generously gave me access to archival family and company material. Karen and Bill Boyd graciously answered my questions and opened their home to me and to my cameras. Edgar Tafel, former apprentice to Wright, was kind enough to write the Introduction, and I thank him for his friendship as well as for invaluable anecdotes and advice. Jonathan Lipman critiqued endless drafts and never hesitated to respond to requests for advice and information.

I owe great thanks to SC Johnson, especially to Cynthia Georgeson, Therese Van Ryne, and Ron Wolter, for allowing me to photograph the nooks and crannies of the Administration Building and Research Tower, and to work on the book in the Great Workroom itself. Gary Wolfe guided me through the Johnson archives. Lois Berg, Boyd Gibbons, and Theresa Henige at Wingspread gave me access to the house.

Charles Montooth, Bruce Brooks Pfeiffer, and especially OsKär Muñoz, at Taliesin and Taliesin West, helped with research requests, and Charles and Minerva Montooth became new friends. Architect Brian A. Spencer, AIA/IAA of Madison, Wisconsin, unselfishly gave me invaluable leads, even if doing so meant that I would be able to publish the results before he might be able to. Chris Paulson, executive director of the Racine Heritage Museum, kept me in good humor and offered valuable suggestions, and Dick Ammann, the museum's archivist, eagerly shared the resources of his treasure trove in the museum basement.

Schindler scholars Judith Sheine and Kathryn Smith helped me with the Monolith Homes. Kurt G. F. Helfrich, curator of the Architecture & Design Collection of the University Art Museum of the University of California, Santa Barbara, provided material about the Monolith Homes project. Anne Marie Smetana, Racine YWCA, gave me access to the 1949 and the 1950 board minutes. Robert Hartmann of Hartmann Design and Jill Hartmann and her colleagues at the Racine Public Library helped as well. Jim and Margaret Yoghourtjian shared resources and their first-rate fresh lemonade and freshly squeezed orange juice, and became new friends.

Anne Sporer Ruetz joyfully shared memories of growing up in the Hardy house. Ken Jesina let me use the Johnson Council House library. The Research Library of The Getty Research Institute in Los Angeles provided copies of correspondence from the Airport commission. Pamela Cassidy Whitenack, archivist for the Hershey Community Archives, helped research J. Mandor Matson's early designs for the SC Johnson Administration Building. Bridget and John Pettinger, owners of the Mitchell house, generously opened their home to my cameras. John Eifler, Brian A. Spencer, Tom Heinz, Rich Johnson, and William Allin Storrer shared their opinions about the Mitchell house. Gerald Karwowski of the Oak Clearing Museum found old photographs for me almost before I had a chance to hang up the phone.

Architect John G. Thorpe of the Frank Lloyd Wright Building Conservancy helped with research about Wright's Chicago and Oak Park days. Lisa Englander and colleagues at the Racine Art Museum shared their library's resources; Russell Maylone and his colleagues at the McCormick Library of Special Collections at Northwestern University and Bruce Renquist of Renquist Associates Incorporated helped with the story of the Miles house.

I thank my employer, The Journal Times, and my newsroom colleagues, including editor Randolph Brandt and photographers Ron Kuenstler and Gregory Shaver, for their support; Dustin Block for giving me the space to publish my findings about the Miles house commission; and especially former city and managing editor Gary Metro for encouraging me to research and write feature stories about Wright in Racine. I must mention the late Ray Kwapil, a Wright devotee who grew up in Racine and became head of the docents at the Meyer May house in Grand Rapids and became a friend as this book was being planned. He died suddenly in 2003, but he is not forgotten.

Cindy Hertzberg, Michael Lee Hertzberg, Boyd Gibbons, and Linda Stengel were copyeditors with sharp eyes. Harvey Riekoff provided computer support. Jim Slosiarek gave me a Pomegranate Frank Lloyd Wright mousepad, which led me to my publisher. I also gratefully acknowledge Katie Burke, Pomegranate's publisher, for supporting this book after seeing only an outline and the very roughest draft of just half a chapter. All the photographs were shot on Fuji color negative film. Much of the book was written to the accompaniment of "The Great Tomato Blues Package, 45 Classic Blues Selections" (1989), Tomato/The Music Works/Rhino Records.

My story about Wright in Racine begins in 1936. Hib Johnson, president of Johnson Wax, asked a friend in advertising to recommend a sculptor to create bas-reliefs of women doing the wash, the ironing, and other house-hold chores, to fit into niches in the new headquarters building for his family owned business. The ad man, who had recently toured Taliesin, Frank Lloyd Wright's home and the site of his Architecture Fellowship in Spring Green, Wisconsin, told Johnson, "You need a good architect, not a sculptor."

In 1932, Wright opened a school—he called it the Taliesin Fellowship—for young architects to tide him over during the lean years of the Great Depression, when building was at a standstill. His apprentices were working on only a few small houses and a school for Wright's aunt. The commission from Johnson was a lifesaver. I joined the Fellowship after one year of architecture at New York University. I intended to stay with Wright just one year, but the one stretched into nine. During those nine years I worked on the Johnson Wax building, the Johnson residence, Fallingwater, and dozens of houses and commercial buildings. I deeply absorbed Wright's principles of using natural materials, opening interiors to the outdoors, avoiding boxy rooms, letting space flow openly throughout the structure, and allowing the exterior to take its own shape rather than follow within the strictures of "Colonial," "Queen Anne," "Victorian," or anything else.

Mark Hertzberg had a brilliant idea when he decided to write about Wright in Racine, because Racine spanned the years of Wright's greatest creativity. His 1905 Thomas Hardy residence violated nearly every architectural rule of its time. Its unadorned facade, which gave no clue to its interior, was half-hidden behind a wall with two widely spaced doors (on which prankish Taliesin students liked to crayon "Boys" and "Girls" on Halloween). However, at the

The barrel chairs at Wingspread are similar to the ones originally designed for the Darwin Martin house complex in Buffalo, New York (1903–1905).

■ ■ ■

rear elevation huge two-story windows provide sweeping views of Lake Michigan. Three decades later the Johnson Wax Building epitomized the open-space principle for office structures, and Wingspread flung out its arms in four directions to accommodate different uses and admit maximum light and views. Readers will be amazed at all the treasures that Hertzberg uncovers and all the insights he offers into the history and the significance of each structure.

While it was my privilege to work on both Wingspread and the Johnson Wax building and in 1940 to carry out my own very first commission in Racine—the lakefront home for the Robert C. Albert family—I learned volumes about Racine and Wright's role in the development of the city from Hertzberg's diligent research, in-depth reconstruction of past personalities and events, loving evocation of the city's architectural riches, and insightful photographs. As Racine enters a new era of business and cultural expansion, it is indeed lucky to have such a perceptive explorer of its storied past!

—Edgar Tafel, FAIA, January 2004

Wright designed the original driveway at Wingspread so that visitors came past the east side
of the house, with its signature balcony cantilevered from Karen Johnson's bedroom.

■ ■ ■

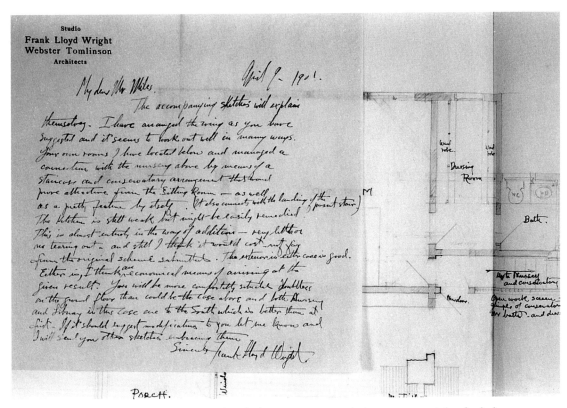

Wright's first known work in Racine was the Miles house. Accompanying this letter were several plans for the house.
Webster Tomlinson was Wright's partner from 1901 to 1902. Photographed by Mark Hertzberg at the
McCormick Library of Special Collections, Northwestern University Library. ▪ ▪ ▪

CECIL CORWIN AND FRANK LLOYD WRIGHT—THE MILES HOUSE (1901)

The prospect of discovering an unknown Frank Lloyd Wright commission is tantalizing. There has been speculation about Wright's rumored authorship of the Mitchell house at 905 Main Street (1894) and about a little-known proposal to remodel the now-demolished Miles house at 2300 Washington Avenue.

Frank Lloyd Wright found both a job and a friend at architect Lyman Silsbee's office when he went to Chicago after dropping out of the University of Wisconsin in 1887. Cecil Corwin, a draftsman, became Wright's close friend

Wright, who was notorious for not paying bills, sent an April 9, 1901, letter to Herbert Miles with 4¢ postage due. Photographed by Mark Hertzberg at the McCormick Library of Special Collections, Northwestern University Library. ■ ■ ■

and confidant, ". . . I'd found a kindred spirit," Wright wrote in his *Autobiography*.[1] Corwin is the thread who ties together the Mitchell and the Miles houses.

The Mitchell house was designed by Corwin, who was listed as the architect of record of several of Wright's "bootleg" houses in Chicago. These were houses that Wright designed when he worked for (Dankmar) Adler and (Louis) Sullivan in Chicago (1887–1893) and was forbidden to accept private commissions. Wright scholars do not accept the Mitchell house as a Wright work.[2] Corwin and Wright shared office space from 1893 until 1896. Architects often trade ideas, and the consensus is that whereas Corwin may have consulted Wright or borrowed some of his ideas for the Mitchell house, Wright did not design the house.

The Miles house, on the other hand, was certified as a Wright project by the Frank Lloyd Wright Foundation, the Wright archive, in 2003.[3] Herbert and Flora Miles wanted to remodel their 1,600-square foot house, which the family called "The Cottage," to create a nursery for their son, Philip Erskine Miles, who was born March 4, 1899. Wright's design for the Miles house is significant, because it shows his attempt to add Prairie-style design elements to a modest 1½-story home. He sent design proposals to the client in April 1901, just three months after he had first formally presented his "Prairie House" concept in the February issue of the *Ladies Home Journal*.

The first record of any remodeling plans for the Miles house is in a letter that Corwin wrote to the Miles family, dated August 7, 1899.[4] Corwin had moved from Chicago to New York City. He sent a sketch of an addition that looks like a smaller version of the Mitchell house, but without its semicircular porch and library, to be built onto the north side of The Cottage.

There is a two-year gap in the Miles house file at Northwestern University; the file resumes with a letter from Wright written April 9, 1901, showing Wright's elevations (drawings) of two designs to remodel the front of the house, and several detailed floor plans. If Wright's handwriting, signature, and return address are not enough to prove his authorship, perhaps the fact that the letter came with 4¢ postage due would convince skeptics—Wright

This sketch shows the long porches that Wright proposed adding to the 1,600-square foot house. The plans also indicate a pinwheel design in the footprint.
Photographed by Mark Hertzberg at the McCormick Library of Special Collections, Northwestern University Library.

■　■　■

was notorious for not paying his bills. The envelope and plans list offices in Oak Park and Chicago for Wright and Webster Tomlinson, Wright's partner from 1901 to 1902.[5]

Unlike Corwin's awkward plan to add a mini-Mitchell house onto the back of the existing Miles home, Wright had a more subtle idea: a pinwheel centered around the existing house. Long porches were proposed for the southeast and northwest ends of the house.[6] The Cottage already extensively used the leaded glass and the casement windows that Wright favored, so he expanded upon them in his remodeling plans.

Robert Hartmann, a designer in Racine, contrasts Wright's design with Corwin's: "Cecil Corwin is still doing period architecture. Wright has already moved out of the bootleg houses into a Prairie house with long, horizontal lines. It does not have a hip roof, but he does not start with a clean sheet of paper.

"He takes a very ordinary gable roofed house and makes it into a personal statement. He has porches extending the length of the house, wrapping around the house. He changes the dormers and integrates them into a new architectural element. . . . It is no longer a period house. He does the opposite of what Corwin did, and puts his own stamp on it.

"He adds wings, he adds porches, but he keeps the basic house to save money. Those drawings show the early beginning of a long linear Prairie house. It is no longer a cottage."[7]

Wright was not completely happy with the designs he sent ("The kitchen is still weak but might be easily remedied"), and welcomed suggestions from Miles. Wright's sense of lighting comes through on a note penned on floor plans for the nursery: "Top light might be let in through screen in ceiling to very good advantage."

Wright's design was never executed. The house was eventually remodeled by Miles' nephew, Malcolm Erskine, about 1928, according to Jean Harris, Erskine's daughter, who lived in the house until 1945. She remembers her mother talking about the Wright design and its long porches.[8] "It's a shame he didn't do it," Harris says, when told more details about the Wright design.

There is a postscript involving Corwin: he married Emma Payne Erskine, Herbert and Flora Miles' sister-in-law, in 1917, nine years after Erskine's death. The Miles-Erskine-Corwin-Wright connection raises a lingering question: Why did Thomas P. Hardy hire Wright in 1905 to build his spectacular house at 1319 Main Street? If we knew whether Hardy was acquainted with Herbert Miles or the Erskines, we might have the answer.

THE HARDY HOUSE (1905)

The Hardy house, a three-story Prairie-style home south of downtown Racine, built for attorney Thomas P. Hardy, dazzled some people and baffled others. In 1905, South Main Street was lined with Classical Revival, Greek Revival, and Italianate houses, the kinds of houses that Frank Lloyd Wright abhorred.[9] In 1893, Daniel H. Burnham, a leading Chicago architect, told Wright that "the Classics" were what Americans wanted, and offered to pay for Wright to study architecture in Europe for six years.[10] There would be a job waiting for him when he returned to Chicago. Wright turned down the lucrative offer, telling Burnham that America needed her own architecture, not imitations of European architecture.

The Hardy house is a symmetrical, rectangular stucco home that stands in stark contrast to the nearby brick and wood-sided homes that try to make a statement with massive columns and often-superfluous ornamentation.

Courtyard gardens are behind the walls at the ends of the Hardy house.

■   ■   ■

A view through Wright's leaded glass windows in the Hardy house reveals conventional turn-of-the-century architecture in the neighborhood. ▪ ▪ ▪

Neighboring houses perch on the top of a bluff overlooking Lake Michigan, facing Main Street, but the Hardy house defied convention by being built into the bluff.

The house turns its back on busy Main Street, showing only the upper half of the home to the public. Its full splendor is on the east or rear side, three stories of glass, stucco, and wood, draped down the upper part of the hill, overlooking the lake. The slender, two-story living room and dining room windows face the lake, with its glorious sunrises and its moody, stormy days.

The Hardy house is different from many of Wright's Prairie designs because of the demands of its narrow lot. Unable to build a sprawling home with an open floor plan, Wright met the topographic challenge by building up and down the bluff. C. E. Percival described the house as "an object of art upon its pedestal" when *House Beautiful* devoted its June 1906 cover to "A House on a Bluff," a flattering story about Hardy house.[11]

Not everyone agreed. Industrialist H. F. Johnson, his family, and friends scoffed at the house, which was five blocks from the Johnson home. They thought it was a "kooky house," and were waiting for it to "fall into the lake," according to Henrietta Louis, Johnson's daughter.[12] She was surprised when her brother, H. F. Johnson Jr., later hired Wright to build his office building (the SC Johnson Administration Building, 1936) and his home (Wingspread, 1937).

Although he disliked basements, Wright included one below the kitchen and dining room level in the Hardy house. Perhaps a basement in a relatively small house on a hill was less objectionable than the traditional basement in a home built on level ground "for the house to sit up on—like a chair."[13]

Some people thought that the house was the beach bathhouse. Anne Sporer Ruetz, who grew up in the house from 1937 to 1947, recalls people coming to their home wanting to change into their bathing suits.[14] The two

Unlike its neighbors, which perch on top of the bluff above Lake Michigan, the Hardy house is actually built into the bluff.

■ ■ ■

doors—originally pocket or sliding doors—are both off Main Street, and Ruetz also remembers pranksters painting "Men" and "Women" on the stucco entryways one Halloween. She says that the family used both doors as front doors; today the north door is the entrance to the house.

Wright designed leaded glass windows and furniture for the Hardy house. An abstraction of the house plan is outlined in white in each of the seven leaded glass windows used in the hallway between the doors.[15]

Six steps lead up from either door to the tall expanse of the living room. The splendor of the living room view is evident, in typically dramatic Wright style, only after one emerges from under the low ceiling of the balcony that

Even the roof over the doorways of the Hardy house has a cantilever.

■ ■ ■

The doorways of the Hardy house (1905), rather than the doors themselves, face Main Street. There were once wood gates across the doorways.

■ ■ ■

Wright abstracted the floor plan of the Hardy house in white in the seven leaded glass windows of the first-floor windows facing Main Street.

■ ■ ■

The full expanse of the living room in the Hardy house is initially hidden by a balcony as one climbs the six steps from the entryway.

■ ■ ■

overlooks the room from the third floor. Ruetz says that her father, Harold Sporer, replaced the original leaded glass windows in the living room, because they "leaked like crazy."[16]

The leaded glass bedroom windows were a source of delight to Ruetz and friends who slept over: "We used to lie in bed and watch the pattern from the car lights come through the leaded glass windows and travel around the room. It was like watching movies."[17] Ruetz also remembers surprising people with the pullout chair in the built-in dresser in her room.[18]

The two-story windows of the Hardy house look out over the lake. The original windows were leaded glass, but Harold Sporer, the second owner of the house, replaced them because they leaked badly.

■ ■ ■

Hardy sold some of the furniture to the Sporers for $75 (equivalent to $960 in 2002)[19] in 1937 when they bought the house. The Bill of Sale lists:

> One Dining Room Table together with two extension ends, and Six Dining Room Chairs with tan leather covered seats, and Two couch beds together with box springs for each bed.
> All of the above pieces made of the knotty parts of Georgia pine, with the exception of the box springs, and designed by Frank Lloyd Wright.[20]

The dining room terrace was added to the Hardy house in 1941.

■ ■ ■

Ruetz used to string a net across the dining room table and play Ping-Pong on the table. The Sporers donated the dining room furniture to a St. Vincent de Paul thrift shop after they sold the house in 1947, because they were unable to find anyone who wanted it, including the new owners of the house. Ruetz says that family members have always wondered if the table ended up as someone's workbench or as firewood.

The Hardy house is not particularly large, the tall living room notwithstanding, but in 1936, the year before the Sporers bought the house, Hardy and Wright corresponded about Hardy's idea to make it into a two-family home. Hardy proposed adding a kitchen to the bedroom on the south side of the dining room, to "give each couple equal cooking facilities" while they both shared the dining room and living room.[21]

A terrace outside the dining room and a recreation room below the basement were added in 1941. The recreation room had a shower for the Sporers and their guests to use after bathing at the nearby beach. In 1941, Wright or one of his draftsmen drew plans—never executed—to add a garage to the north side of the house, perhaps by tearing down the house next door.[22]

In 1905, when the hill below the house was relatively barren, diagonal paths led to the beach below, and a swimming pool was fed from the lake.[23] No trace of the pool exists anymore. The hill has filled with trees that help shade the house in summer and also block the most spectacular view of the house in the almost 100 years since the house was built.

WINGSPREAD (1937)

Supposedly H. F. Johnson Jr. had told Frank Lloyd Wright that "The [Administration] building is so beautiful and attractive that I think I'll just put a cot in my office and live here," to which Wright replied, "Oh, no you won't, I'll build you a house."[24] Wright did, indeed. Wingspread is as dramatic and breathtaking a home as the Johnson Administration Building is an office building, "a constant dance of sunshine and shadows."[25]

Johnson and Wright were only four months into the construction of the Administration Building when Johnson talked to Wright about building him a new home. In November 1936 he showed Wright farmland that he owned in Wind Point, just north of the city of Racine. Johnson, who was divorced and had two children, married Jane Roach, who also had two children, on New Year's Eve. The "Homestead," as their 1902 Gothic Revival home at

When Wright was designing Wingspread, he asked Johnson's daughter, Karen, 13, what features she would like in the house. She wanted a cantilevered balcony like the one she had seen at Taliesin. ■   ■   ■

Wright called the living room—the central part of the zoned Wingspread house—the wigwam because the the room was shaped like a teepee. One of the five fireplaces in the thirty-foot-high chimney tower is shown here.

■   ■   ■

1739 Wisconsin Avenue is still known, was too small for the new family, and the couple visited Wright soon after the wedding to talk about a new house.

Johnson had recently visited the Drake Hotel in Chicago, and had been impressed by the main lobby, a two-story-high open space, under a skylight, with openings in the surrounding walls leading to other areas of the hotel, including the Palm Court.[26] The Palm Court was another open space, with a fireplace as its focal point.

Wright had explained his idea for a zoned house to Johnson while they walked the land in Wind Point. Unlike the Prairie concept, in which rooms were more likely to flow into one another, a zoned home would have distinct, separate, and quiet private spaces flowing from the central family gathering space.

This aerial view shows the dramatic, zoned house—Wingspread —that Wright designed for H. F. Johnson Jr. in 1937.
It was the architect's last Prairie home, and his largest.

■　■　■

When they met with Wright, the Johnsons brought a sketch that Mr. Johnson had made, showing a cross-shaped home with four zoned wings jutting from a square, central space. Johnson proposed a master bedroom wing, children's bedroom wing, a kitchen and servants' wing, and a garage wing with guest bedrooms.

Wright sited the house on a rise above a series of ponds. He offset the wings, making a pinwheel, rather than a cross, but otherwise kept Johnson's design. The centerpiece was the living room, which he called the "wigwam," after a teepee-like room with four fireplaces in an unbuilt design for the Nakoma Country Club in Madison (1924).[27] The Wingspread wigwam, like the house itself, was designed with four zones on the different sides of the chimney tower: the "Entrance Hall," the dining room, the living room, and a library living room. All rooms would be sunlit.[28]

Sunlight spills across the massive chimney through the myriad clerestory windows above Wingspread's wigwam. ▪ ▪ ▪

The pinwheel made the center of the house a true resting place, rather than the busy crossroads of the house.[29]

The small and unobtrusive front door leads to a foyer with a six-foot-high ceiling.[30] Then, as in the Hardy house, the Administration Building, and the Keland house, one emerges from under the low ceiling into nothing less than the breathtaking soul of the building.

The hearth was generally the centerpiece of Wright's houses, perhaps nowhere as dramatically as at Wingspread. Five fireplaces were built into the massive thirty-foot-high oval chimney, four on the first floor, and one on the mezzanine.

The octagonal living room is crowned by three rows of skylights surrounding the chimney. The chimney tower is evocative of the curved lines of the Administration Building, in stark contrast to the straight lines of the four wings or zones of the house.

Much of the oak furniture in the wigwam is built in, but freestanding pieces, such as end tables and hassocks, are octagonal, like the room itself.[31] Edgar Tafel, the apprentice assigned to supervise construction of Wingspread, suggested the barrel chairs modeled after the ones Wright had designed for the Darwin Martin house in Buffalo

The gardens are an important part of Wingspread's grounds.

■ ■ ■

(1904).[32] The Wingspread chairs are smaller, flex less, and are not as comfortable as those in the Martin house, Tafel says, because of changes Wright made to the design.

Wright had a dramatic vision for the driveway, and brought visitors in from the east from Lighthouse Drive. The driveway was closed when Wingspread became a conference center in 1959, and it is now a nature walk. Today visitors approach Wingspread's driveway from the north, from Four Mile Road. Instead of seeing Wingspread rise dramatically from its surroundings as Wright had intended, the visitors' first view of the house is of a residence that sits on level ground.

Jonathan Lipman, an architect who has studied the house extensively, captures the essence of Wright's vision for

The spiral staircase at Wingspread snakes up the chimney tower from the mezzanine to the Crow's Nest.

■ ■ ■

the house: "The necessary thing to understand about Wingspread is that the way you were to approach the building was very important to Wright, and carefully orchestrated by him. . . . It [Wright's driveway] creates a circuitous route. You glimpse the building, then veer away from it around a large pond, and then swing back around and catch the building behind the pond, and you continue to approach the house in a tightening spiral. The effect is that the building seems to be spiraling around you. It's a brilliant optical illusion that gives the impression that the building is moving.

"As one approaches the building via this preferred driveway, the second story wing of the house appears to hover over the pond. When approached with the pond in the foreground, the house is like the wings of great Canada geese that are circling the water. It is as though the house itself was flying off the site like a Canada goose. It's as powerful a piece of poetry as has been written into any building. . . . But the organic relationship between the building and water goes further. Wright actually placed Wingspread over the spring which fed the pond below. So, to the Johnson family who knew well this spring, it was as though the house itself springs out of the spring. It is built poetry."[33]

Johnson's daughter, now Karen Johnson Boyd, looks at a recent photograph of Canada geese nesting just outside her father's former bedroom and says, "He would have loved to open his eyes and see them sitting there. One of his favorite things was to make sure they got fed."[34]

Karen, then 13, and her brother, Sam, 9, suggested two of the building's signature features. Wright had written them, asking if there was anything they wanted included in the house.[35] Karen, whose bedroom was at the north end of the house, on the second floor past the master bedrooms, requested a cantilevered balcony like the dramatic one she had seen at Taliesin.[36] Wright told her that some day she would be wooed from below the balcony by a suitor "with a classical guitar, of course."[37] The bedroom placement was not ideal—"I had to sneak past my father's door if I wanted to sneak out."

The children loved the spectacular view from the cupola of their maternal grandmother's house in Ithaca, New York, and they asked Wright for a similar lookout

The Crow's Nest at Wingspread, designed for Johnson's children, dominates the top of the chimney. ▪ ▪ ▪

tower in their new home.[38] Wright gave them the Crow's Nest, a glass enclosure next to the chimney, which is reached by a spiral staircase from the mezzanine above the wigwam. It was a child's delight. The children could see the lake, watch their father, an avid pilot, fly past the house, and they could leave each other notes in a locked cabinet. The key was lost, and Karen wonders if there is still a forgotten note in the cabinet. Sam enjoyed playing "Capture the Flag" games there with his friends.

Wright told Karen that one day a suitor would serenade her as she stood on her balcony.

■   ■   ■

When he was supervising the construction, Tafel made two significant decisions that would have incurred Wright's wrath, but he managed to keep one secret from Wright. He and Wes Peters, Wright's son-in-law, did not think that the cantilever under Karen's bedroom was strong enough.[39] They suggested to Johnson that he think about adding a storeroom at the north end of the first floor (one in which they could hide steel beams that they hoped Wright would never know about). When Johnson agreed to the suggestion, they went to Wright and told him that Johnson had asked for a storeroom. Wright told them to add it. They intended to add two steel beams, but only one was found during building repairs in 1967.[40]

Wright was in the Soviet Union when Tafel agreed with the contractor's suggestion that the sewer line on the south side of the house should be moved away from the house, in case it ever needed repair. As a result, the pool had to be relocated as well. Wright was "furious" when he visited the construction site and learned of the change. Tafel recalls, "I backed up from him and fell into the pool trench. He looked at me and said, 'You got what you deserved!'"[41]

Karen's balcony is framed by the tidewater red cypress Wright selected for the construction of Wingspread.

∎   ∎   ∎

Wingspread was well known for its leaky roof, perhaps more so because of a story Sam Johnson tells[42] about the first big dinner party, given only after his father thought that the leaks had been fixed. Guests included a senator and the governor. Young Sam, now 13, was allowed to sit at the edge of the dining room. It started to rain and the roof leaked. Rain splashed off H. F.'s (bald) head.

H. F. was seething, and demanded that the telephone be brought to the table. He told the operator that he wanted to talk to Frank Lloyd Wright at Taliesin West in Scottsdale, Arizonia. When Wright came on the line, H. F. told him that he was giving an important dinner party and that rain was leaking on his head. He asked "Frank" what he intended to do. Wright had one suggestion. The answer was loud enough for all the guests to hear: "Well, Hib, why don't you move your chair?"

Sam Johnson (second from right) helps lower an aluminum alloy beam used to replace damaged wood beams when Wingspread's roof was repaired, November 22, 1996.

■   ■   ■

Sam says that the legendary leak was discussed almost sixty years later, when the Johnson Foundation was planning an extensive roof renovation and replacement: "Do we leave the leak that came down on my father's head? I knew exactly where it was."[43] The leak was fixed. Johnson says of the repairs, "I'm glad we preserved it for Wingspread, for my father, and kept it pretty much the way it was."

Karen vividly recalls that two of the innovations in the house were dismal failures.[44] One was the dining room table, which could be pulled back into the butler's pantry, so that dishes might be removed and the next course set. "The worst thing was that some women had taken their shoes off under the table. My grandmother . . . asked, 'What's the matter with the people in the kitchen. Can't they come out and clean the table, Hibbard?'"

The back of Wingspread—shown here in winter—has been photographed so often that many people think it is the front of the house.

■   ■   ■

And then there were the twelve-foot-long logs stacked vertically in some of the tall fireplaces in the wigwam— "Those great wonderful long birch logs. They burned beautifully. We knew what was going to happen, my dad, Sam, and I. As they started burning [from the bottom] they fell [into the room], and we had to get the tongs and throw them outside on the patio below, and everyone congratulated themselves on not getting burned."

Jane Roach died suddenly while Wingspread was under construction. Johnson was grieving deeply and lost his enthusiasm for the house.[45] Wright urged him to continue with the project. Johnson remarried in October 1941, but his new wife, Irene Purcell, a former movie actress to whom he was married for more than thirty years, sensed that the house wasn't built for her.

Dramatic fifteen-foot-high living room
windows at Wingspread overshadow
the entryway at the right.

■   ■   ■

Wingspread is a dazzling cornucopia of shapes and lines, as shown in this dramatic view of the Crow's Nest.

■ ■ ■

Many pieces of sculpture are situated on the grounds of Wingspread, now home to the Johnson Foundation.

■ ■ ■

Another legendary story occured before dawn, when Wright was an overnight guest. Wright liked to orchestrate every aspect of his homes. He took in Irene Purcell's Wingspread and then took it apart, Karen remembers.[46]

"He took paintings down and put them in the closet. He put some of her furniture into the closet, too. It was very naughty. Then he sat down at the piano when he was done and played Chopin and woke them up. Father came out and said, 'Frank, do you know what time it is?'" Wright was unmoved. "I thought a little music would be soothing to you and help you sleep better."

Karen continues, "The first time he just made suggestions about things, and the second time he carried them out. And she [Mrs. Johnson] said, 'I hope I never see you here again.' She told my father that Wingspread was too big for them and not a place she wanted to live. Part of it . . . it was designed for another woman." The Johnsons commissioned Henry L. Eggers to design a new home, which would become known as The House, just east of Wingspread, in 1956.

H. F. established the Johnson Foundation to sponsor conferences about local, regional, national, and international issues. Wingspread was given to the Foundation in 1959. National Public Radio, the National Endowment of the Arts, the Frank Lloyd Wright Building Conservancy, and the International Court of Justice all evolved from Wingspread conferences.

The Johnson family and the Foundation had a new challenge: how to preserve Wingspread while turning it into a conference center. Climate control was a concern, for example. The unreliable radiant floor heating system that Wright had designed, a system that was ahead of its time because zoned climate controls had not yet been developed, would be inadequate for a conference center, so a new heating and air-conditioning system was installed.

Bedrooms and the Terrace Room playroom became meeting rooms. A business executive's Shangri-La now nurtured guests from all over the world as they gathered to find common ground for solving problems and fashioning creative solutions for myriad issues.

Since 1958, there have been almost a dozen proposals to modify Wingspread or to add new buildings next to it.[47] The most dramatic proposal, made in 1960, was to add a dining hall, an auditorium, a chapel, and a motel for conferees, connected to the west wing.[48] Plans that would have altered the look of Wingspread and the balance of the campus were all scuttled.

The Foundation outgrew its office space in Wingspread's former garage and guestroom wing; an office building, named for Karen Johnson Boyd, was built across from The House in 1990. The forty-two-room Guesthouse was built east of those new offices in 2002.

Wright drew plans in 1938 for a gatehouse and a farm for the property, and he and H. F. Johnson Jr. discussed building an airplane hangar and landing strip.[49] None of the ideas materialized.

Sam Johnson once asked Wright to name his greatest building. Wright replied, "The next one, young Johnson, always the next one."[50] Still, Wright was obviously proud of Wingspread when he told a British audience, "This is probably one of the most complete, best constructed and most expensive houses it has ever been my good fortune to build."[51]

THE ROY PETERSEN HOUSE (1941)

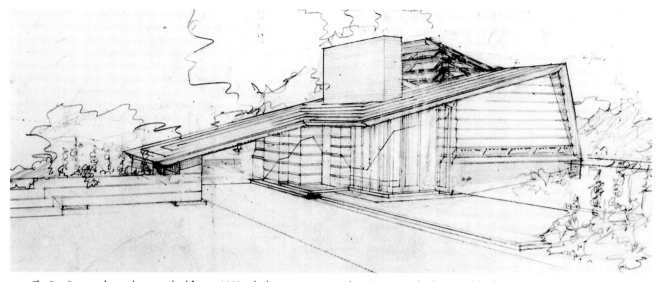

The Roy Petersen house design evolved from a 1939 unbuilt commission in northern Wisconsin. The design was finally executed by Charles Montooth, a former apprentice to Wright, for a client in Ann Arbor, Michigan, in 1979. It was known as the Whitford-Haddock house.

It took forty years, three clients, and two architects for this Usonian design to be realized. Wright originally designed the home in 1939 for Edith Carlson, a schoolteacher who lived in Superior, in northern Wisconsin, but it was not built.[52] Wright called the home "Below Zero," and made a drawing showing it covered by snow. There was very little exposed glass because of the sometimes-brutal winter weather in Superior. The sloping roof was designed to protect the home from heavy snow and extreme cold.

Two years later Wright reprised the design for a proposed home in Racine. The client was Roy Petersen, a photographer for SC Johnson. Petersen had taken photographs for Wright, including the early photographs of the Broadacre City model.[53] The Petersen house was never built, either.

The design was finally built in 1979 for Fred Haddock in Ann Arbor, Michigan, under the supervision of Charles Montooth, who joined the Taliesin Fellowship in 1945 and worked with the Taliesin Associated Architects from 1959, when Wright died, until the partnership was restructured in 2003.

THE KELAND HOUSE (1954)

The Keland house, shown in this aerial view, was designed by Wright in 1954 for H. F. Johnson's daughter, Karen Johnson Keland. John Howe built an addition in 1961.

■   ■   ■

Almost fifty years after he designed the Hardy house, Wright designed a home for H. F. Johnson Jr.'s daughter, then Karen Johnson Keland. The residence is located on the bluff of a ravine that overlooks the Root River and Colonial Park. Karen says that she picked Wright to design her own home in 1954 "because I lived in Wingspread and loved it." Her father was less sure about her choice of architect because he knew what it was like to commission a Wright building, and he was afraid that it would be too expensive. Johnson wrote Wright, asking him to recommend an architect. Karen recalls Wright's answer: "Of course I can recommend someone, but wouldn't it be better for the daughter to have the real thing? I would love to do a house for Karen."[54] He got the commission, but her father warned her to be careful.

The living room of the Keland house as viewed from Colonial Park, across the Root River.

■　■　■

The Keland house living room is cantilevered above the ravine; it looks out over the Root River.

■   ■   ■

The Keland house living room is filled with art and is arranged in two sections.

■ ■ ■

It is almost inconceivable to think of Wright agreeing to have another architect looking over his shoulder, but Karen says that he did not balk when Johnson assigned John Halama, the company architect, to supervise the job.[55] Halama and Wright had already worked together on the Johnson Research Tower and other projects.[56] When the Kelands also hired consultants from Indiana University to help design the home's radiant heating system—something Karen's father recommended because of problems with Wingspread's system—she says that "Mr. Wright never said 'boo' about it . . . I think Mr. Wright was relieved he didn't have to do it."[57]

Wright may have been on his best behavior when the house was being built, but he was true to form when he and Wes Peters came for lunch in 1956 after the Kelands had moved in. Karen had fixed one of her favorite guest lunches: chicken salad, with curry in the mayonnaise; buttered toast broiled with sesame seeds; and green grapes.

She served Coca-Colas to her guests after lunch, at which time Wright decided that it was time to rearrange the furniture.[58]

"I knew it was to be expected because he had already done it to Irene [Purcell Johnson] and dad at Wingspread, famously, in the middle of the night without asking permission." Her stepmother had also warned her: "Just remember, Karen, he's going to come back and rearrange everything."

The only furnishings that Wright had designed for the Keland house were built-ins: ledges, bookcases, cabinets, and two sofas. The living room furniture was arranged in two groupings, because the family did not often entertain large groups of people. Wright said that he liked the two beige Moroccan rugs, and asked where they were from. Then he turned his attention to the furniture. He had Peters move the baby grand piano into the center of the room because the Keland children were taking piano lessons and he thought that the family should gather around the piano every night.[59]

A garden courtyard is situated between the three wings of the Keland house. ▪ ▪ ▪

Karen remembers Wright asking, "Do you mind if I show you the way I think? I like your furniture and your rugs and the drapes. You've done a great job, but I think you have to arrange it in a more family way." It was part of his persona. "He was laughing and grinning, he was getting a kick out of it," Karen recalls. "Even Wes Peters was laughing. 'Don't worry about it,' he whispered, 'This is just in fun' as he was pushing and shoving things around." Karen knew not to argue. "I thanked him for it and said we'll try it out and see how it works. It stayed that way for a couple of days. It just didn't look right."[60]

From the courtyard, visitors can look through the living room windows of the Keland house to the trees in the ravine.

■   ■   ■

The entryway at the Keland house leads to the open dining room and to the living room, which faces the ravine.

■ ■ ■

Visitors to the Keland house enter into a garden courtyard under a low copper roof, passing between a garage on the left and the former carport on the right. In 1961, John Howe, Wright's chief draftsman for many years, added the garage when the carport was remodeled into additional living space. A diagonal walkway, added at the same time, leads to the present front door, a bit to the left of the original door.

The Keland house is larger than most of Wright's Usonian homes, but it has many characteristics of the Usonian designs. The original house was L shaped, with a third wing for the carport. The dining area, with its two-ton Vermont marble table that took fifteen men to carry into the house, is just off the entry hall, and flows into the living room.[61] The living room dominates the main wing; it is spacious, and comfortable, filled with books and art. The built-in furnishings are also an important part of the Usonian design concept.

The kitchen "work space" is at the hinge of the Keland house, between the living room and the bedroom wings. The folding wood doors—fashioned after Wright's original wood screen—hide the wet bar. ▪ ▪ ▪

The Keland house kitchen is at the "hinge" between the living room/dining room wing and the bedroom wing, following the Usonian model. Wright, who normally didn't seem to worry about what other people thought, suggested a wood screen to hide a small wet bar that adjoins the kitchen—"What are you going to do when the minister comes?"[62]

The bedrooms are in the south wing. The hallway is narrower than Wright had wanted, because Karen requested built-in storage cabinets along the outside wall. She also insisted on a basement, a feature that Wright termed "unwelcome" in his definition of organic architecture in his *Autobiography*.[63] The guestroom is on the second floor of the main wing, adjoining a sitting room, which overlooks the living room and the ravine below.

Wright wanted to include a cantilever in the design, jutting out from the guestroom, like the one he designed for Karen's bedroom at Wingspread. It was eliminated from the final house plans, for budgetary reasons, to Karen's regret: "It would have been a very distinctive part of the house."[64]

A sitting room on the balcony overlooks the living room and part of the dining room at the Keland house. ▪ ▪ ▪

Karen loved the Wright home she grew up in, and loves the one she commissioned. "Depending on your mood, it expands with you or contracts. You can go in a little cozy eating area in the kitchen, or if you feel expansive you come out here [the living room] and have a great big party if you want."[65]

Her son, Bill Keland, was just 1 year old when the family moved into the house, but it had a great influence on him.[66] The land itself was a child's delight—"We used to live down on that river, and play on that river . . . that whole valley was our playground. We had our bikes, we caught fish. That was where we lived most of the year. It was a great place to grow up." His classmates knew that there was something different about the house: "They would look around and wonder what kind of place they were in, with its long hallways, and low ceilings opening up into a big room."

Wright's design moves Bill Keland even today and influenced the design of his own home in California. "It [the Keland house] always felt like it was a sacred space, thought out space. It made me feel like a human being."

Karen's husband, Bill Boyd, moved to Racine when he became president of the Johnson Foundation at Wingspread in 1980. He recalls his introduction to Wright's work: "I went out to Wingspread and I was absolutely smitten."[67] Next, he was interviewed by Sam Johnson in his office in the Administration Building, a building "that is like a festival the

The layout of the Keland house is similar to the scheme of Wright's smaller Usonian homes, although the house was constructed of brick rather than wood. The room to the left was added in 1961. ▪ ▪ ▪

way it opens up to you." He was hooked. "I had two Frank Lloyd Wright experiences in my first day and was smitten." He was invited to dinner at Karen's house after starting his new job. "Then I married into the house. I often think she must think I married her for the house, I love it so much."

Frank Lloyd Wright once again brought together nature and the house in this spacious, two-story home designed five years before he died. The Boyds enjoy watching the river and the birds that flock to the courtyard garden. Bill pauses on the stairs of the house, looking out an east window over a ravine, as he takes a visitor through the home on a late fall day, pointing out a nut hatch sitting in a tree just outside the window. "This is what I love about living in this house."[68]

The house is filled with art. To Karen, it *is* art—"Sometimes I feel like I'm living in a piece of sculpture."[69]

The Administration Building commission helped to redefine Wright's career in 1936 as much as it helped to define the Johnson company. It was followed by the Research Tower commission (1944), which was Wright's first chance to build his tap-root tower design. ▪ ▪ ▪

SC JOHNSON ADMINISTRATION BUILDING (1936)

Frank Lloyd Wright's homes opened themselves to the surrounding landscape. Many of his public buildings, by contrast, were introverted, shutting out their surroundings and celebrating the interior space instead. The Larkin Building in Buffalo, New York (built in 1903, demolished in 1950) and the Unity Temple and Meeting House in Oak Park (1905) formed the foundation that Wright elaborated upon when he designed the SC Johnson Administration Building in 1936.

The Administration Building's clerestory windows accent the famous Cherokee red bricks.
▪ ▪ ▪

Close up of the Administration Building's Pyrex tube windows.
▪ ▪ ▪

There are many layers to the story of the Administration Building. The building's "dendriform" (tree-shaped, but commonly called mushroom-shaped) columns are legendary, as are the forty-three miles of Pyrex tube windows, and the Steelcase furniture that Wright designed. The story of the Administration Building is also the story of the start of a special relationship between a forward-looking client and his iconoclastic architect.

The Administration Building is stunning, an edifice of circles and curves, inside and out. One cannot help but notice new details at every visit. The Cherokee red bricks come in some two hundred shapes—mostly curved—and the building flows around the Great Workroom like a gentle stream. It is the antithesis of the traditional office building that was initially proposed by J. Mandor Matson, a Racine architect.[1]

Although international accolades have been showered on the Administration Building since it opened in 1939, it almost was not built. The company was close to breaking ground on a design by Matson, but he lost the commission weeks before the scheduled groundbreaking after H. F. Johnson Jr., chairman and president of the company, met Wright on July 20, 1936.[2]

The Johnson archives show plans for three designs by Matson, two from 1935 and another "Drawn J.M.M. Mar. 16. 1936."[3] The first 1935 plan was simply a proposal to remodel an existing building; the other two plans were for a completely new building. The different plans may indicate the uncertainty with which Johnson executives viewed Matson's designs. They accepted Wright's initial proposal immediately.

Blueprints in the Johnson archives, and a sketch by Edgar Tafel, who supervised construction of the Administration Building, offer a glimpse of what might have been built at 1525 Howe Street instead of the Wright building. Tafel, an apprentice to Wright from 1932 to 1941, drew a copy of one of Matson's proposals for the Johnson building from memory in 1995, in preparation for a lecture.[4]

Johnson had suggested that Matson look at the Hershey Chocolate Company's new Art Moderne air-conditioned office building in Hershey, Pennsylvania.[5] He also wanted Matson to decorate the building in some way to tell the story of the company's products.[6]

The Johnson and Hershey companies were both owned by families who were keenly interested in their employees' welfare. The idea of air-conditioning was particularly important to Johnson, who would close the company for the day if temperatures in the factory reached 90 degrees.[7]

Some of Matson's blueprints indicate a Classical Revival entrance; others show touches of the Moderne style that was popular at the time. Matson's final proposal for the main entrance of the new building included a doorway flanked on each side by three bas-relief sculptures featuring Johnson products in use: a woman waxing a floor, a child waxing a table, and a man painting mechanical equipment.[8]

Matson had made three sets of plans, a year apart, but neither Johnson nor key company managers were happy with the design, even though they were about to break ground. Whereas Johnson wanted the new building to "eliminate the drabness and dullness we so often find in office buildings,"[9] Matson proposed a building that was as dull as the Wright design is challenging, exciting, and innovative. Tafel bluntly called it "terrible."[10]

Serge Logan, the company's former director of communications, says that Matson's building "looked like a salt cracker box to most of the people who were there; square, with not much character to it."[11] Wright characterized Matson's design as "a fancy crematorium."[12] Jack Ramsey, the company's general manager, was told to keep looking for architects after telling Johnson that the Matson design "isn't good enough, it's just another building."[13]

Ramsey and William Connolly, Johnson's advertising manager, had shown Matson's plans to Melvin Brorby, the company's public relations consultant, and E. Willis Jones, Brorby's artist, in Chicago. They said that they were looking for a sculptor for the bas-relief sculptures or for a frieze at the top of the building; they were told that "You don't need an artist, you need a good architect."[14]

Jones was "horrified" by Matson's design, and "couldn't believe that we would build such a building." Jones recently had spent a weekend with Wright at Taliesin, and was "absolutely charmed by him."[15] He took Connolly and Ramsey to Spring Green to meet Wright. That Friday night, July 17, 1936, after talking with Wright, Ramsey was bursting with excitement and couldn't wait to tell Johnson about him.[16] Johnson was at his cottage on Lake Owen in northern Wisconsin, but Ramsey resisted the urge to send him "wild telegrams" or to call him right away.[17] Instead, he stopped at work on his way to church Sunday morning, "to the peace and quiet of the office," to write Johnson a ten-page handwritten letter. What a letter it was—one that shaped the future of the company and helped spark the revival of Wright's dormant architectural practice.

Wright's practice had been in such bad shape by 1932 that he and his wife, Olgivanna, had formed the Taliesin Fellowship, an apprentice program for architects, at their home near Spring Green. The year 1936 was particularly bad. Fifty years later Olgivanna Lloyd Wright recalled that "1936 was a lean year for Taliesin. We had felt the effects of the depression that gripped the country and though our work and expenses went on, architectural commissions were very few. Frank Lloyd Wright attacked this new project [the Johnson commission] with the greed of a man starved for work."[18]

In his *Autobiography,* Wright himself was more poetic about the commission. "When the sky at Taliesin was dark, the days there gloomy, as I have described them, Hib [Johnson's nickname] and Jack were the ones who came out to Taliesin one day to see about that new building. They came, you might say, like messengers riding on white steeds trumpeting glad tidings [after getting a $10,000 retainer from Johnson] . . . the birds began to sing, sing again

Edgar Tafel drew a sketch of what might have been the Johnson office building if company executives had not met Frank Lloyd Wright. The local architect lost his commission the day after H. F. Johnson Jr. met Wright. Photograph used with permission of Edgar Tafel. ▪ ▪ ▪

below the home at Taliesin; dry grass on the hillside waxed green; the hollyhocks went gaily into a second blooming . . . Taliesin galvanized into fresh activity. A good commission!"[19] Wright was never wanting for work again.

Ramsey wrote Johnson, "We have right here under our noses, a native Wisconsinian (sic), who was the absolute father of all modern architecture, who is the outstanding architect of the world today . . . and it would be a crime not to talk to him."[20] He added, "gosh he could tell us what we were after when we couldn't explain it ourselves."[21] Ramsey also wrote that Wright had looked at Matson's plans and told Ramsey that the niches for the sculptures "memorialized the defunct windows," meaning that Matson evidently could not forget that windows had to be in a building whether it were windowless or not."[22] Wright proposed to give Johnson far more for $200,000 than Matson had proposed building for $300,000.[23]

Ramsey even touched on the bad publicity that had engulfed Wright and stalled his career, imploring Johnson, "Don't think of newspaper publicity on his matrimonial troubles and all that, right away as I did. That all means nothing in regard to architecture of course."[24] Ramsey wrote, "Got to stop and get to church" at the end of his breathless note, the note that led to a turning point for both Wright and the Johnson company.[25]

Stewart Macaulay, Ramsey's son-in-law, interprets the note to Johnson as a bold one.[26] "Undoubtedly, he was excited about the chance to get Wright, but also he had to be 101% for it so that Hib might accept his recommendation. Jack had to get Hib to see it as Hib's project."

The Great Workroom is the centerpiece of the Administration Building. Wright said that the Administration Building was an offspring of the Larkin Building (1903), in which he pioneered his concept of a vast, open office workplace. ■ ■ ■

Johnson drove to Taliesin. Johnson, the free-spirited businessman, and Wright, the free-spirited architect, did not agree on many things when they first met, but they found that they had one thing in common: they both drove stylish, streamlined Lincoln Zephyrs. "He had a Lincoln-Zephyr (sic), and I had one—that was the only thing we agreed on. On all other things we were at each other's throats."[27]

Jonathan Lipman, author of the definitive study of the Administration Building, says that the Zephyr was an important symbol of the Johnson-Wright relationship. "Streamlining was associated with the recent triumphs of technology over nature in craft [such as] airplanes and ocean liners. Seeing that the other man shared this portentous car likely reinforced to each other that the other man, like himself, understood and was a part of this grand new triumphant epoch of progress."[28]

Wright told Johnson that he had built "a far better administrative building [the Larkin Building] 30 years earlier."[29] Wright later characterized the Johnson building as the "daughter of the Larkin Building," a "more feminine building" than "its sire, the masculine Larkin Building of Buffalo."[30] Johnson was not thin-skinned. On the contrary, he thought, "If that guy can talk like that he must have something."[31] In 1956, Johnson said in a broadcast interview, "So I tried to insult him back but it is pretty hard work!"[32]

Although Johnson and Wright disagreed about many things, including where to locate the new building, they began a long relationship that led to the designs of the Administration Building (1936); Wingspread, the Johnson home (1937); the SC Johnson Research Tower (1944); the Keland House, designed for Johnson's daughter, Karen (1954); and several unbuilt projects, including a new YWCA building (1949, 1950).

Even Johnson's then-12-year-old daughter Karen understood what a great architect Wright was: "I just remember the time right after dad first saw Mr. Wright, I was at Kemper Hall [a boarding school in nearby Kenosha], and he came down to pick me up one Sunday and he said to me, 'Karen, you're studying art history, now who is the greatest

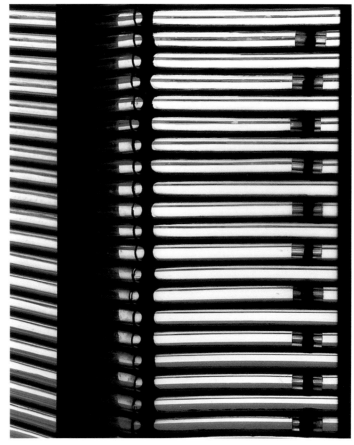

Some sections of the mezzanine above the entryway have walls made of glass tubes.

architect in America?'" She was sitting next to her father in the front seat of his cream-colored Lincoln convertible, and replied, "Why everybody knows it's Frank Lloyd Wright.'"[33] "He was sort of appalled that I knew that. I remember that vividly. He was flabbergasted that his kid would know it. He told me at that time that he was going to have Mr. Wright do the building."

J. Mandor Matson had worked on his designs for more than two years, but he was told to stop just four days after Ramsey wrote his note to Johnson.[34]

Tafel vividly remembers Wright's draftsmen and apprentices working feverishly on the Johnson plans after they were hired.[35] "We were given drawings, a plot plan. We had seen Matson's drawings. That building was interesting because there were no windows as such, it was to be air conditioned. There were very few air conditioned buildings. There was enough information as to which people would be working in the Administration Building and also there would be offices for the heads of departments. . . . So from that Wright came up with a scheme for the building, and we worked day and night on this for what must have been two weeks. I remember doing a lot of the important drawings. He had me make a very special drawing where he had me take the back of the building off where you saw the stairs, the second floor, the whole thing."

One can imagine the panic that the apprentices felt in the drafting room at Taliesin when they came in one morning and realized that someone forgot to turn off one of the 35-watt lightbulbs over the drafting table, and it had exploded. "The red hot metal fell on the drawing, and it all burned up." Tafel redid the drawing.

Wright went to his vault next to the drafting room the night before the apprentices finished and took out Japanese prints to give to each of them. Tafel still has his hanging in his Greenwich Village townhouse. "It is beautiful."[36]

Wright ordered Tafel to take him to Racine for a meeting with Johnson executives after the preliminary drawings were finished. "Edgarrrrr, get dressed, put a suit on, we're going to Racine!"[37] Tafel took the roll of building plans from the backseat when they arrived, put them under his arm, and started to follow Wright. Wright grabbed them from him, saying, "The architect carries his own plans."[38]

There was no question who dominated the meeting, Tafel recalls—"He [Wright] took the position that he was the Lord, and that he was making a presentation of a work of art to be used in the future, and how the people would be seeing each other working. . . . The roof did not go out to cover over the outside wall, and we had the big band of skylights and between the columns would be skylight. In the morning when you get there the sun will be coming up, and all day long they'll see where the sun is. If there's a storm, we'll turn on the lights on the inside. It was a great thing, a new approach to everything is how Wright pitched it. Those people were so pleased, they were all smiling. They realized they were in a very important moment in their personal lives, and that's where we found that Wright had a way of designing for use, for people, for the subject."[39]

The apprentices were equally moved. "We were so thrilled. Most of the other things had been just one or two houses. We weren't making drawings for big things of this nature. We just thought it was great." More than six decades later, Tafel still characterizes Wright's performance with awe: "He was the greatest salesman in the world."[40]

Tafel lived across the street from the construction site for two years while he supervised the job. He still bristles at not having been invited to the opening.[41] He surmises that "I don't think he (Wright) wanted to give anyone credit."

Wright disdained the south side neighborhood surrounding the Johnson property.[42] He had tried to persuade Johnson to adopt a variation of his Broadacre plan, a vision of an entire community outside Racine, including

The Administration Building and the Research Tower glow at dusk, as light shimmers through the miles of glass tube windows.

■ ■ ■

housing for employees as well as the company building. Johnson did not want to move the company.[43] Wright's wife, Olgivanna, warned her husband that he might lose the commission if he continued to argue for the Broadacre City concept, so Wright concentrated on designing a building that was exciting on the inside.

Wright downplayed the building's location by placing a carport and the main entrance on the north side of the building, away from busy 16th Street, which the south side of the building faced. Entering the building from the carport fit in with Wright's Broadacre concept.[44] The automobile was an essential tool in decentralizing society without isolating people.[45]

On New Year's Eve, *The Racine Journal Times* previewed the building in a big splash on the front page.[46] The story referred to "an office building with 'windowless walls'"; "shadowless illumination"; and "columns like golf tees." Wright was quoted: "This new building will be simply and sincerely an interpretation of modern business conditions designed to be as inspiring to live in and work in as any cathedral ever was to worship in."[47]

Construction of the Administration Building began before Wright had finalized the window scheme.
He had to invent the racks that held the tubes in place during construction.

■　■　■

Air-conditioned buildings like the Hershey and Johnson buildings no longer needed traditional windows that could be opened in warm weather.[48] Matson's building presumably was to be lit entirely by artificial lighting, while Wright looked for ways to let the sun light the building.[49]

Wright wanted to fill his building with indirect lighting from skylights and the now signature forty-three miles of Pyrex tubing. Gray days are the norm during Racine's winters, and Ramsey asked Wright how any work would get done when the sun was not shining.[50] Wright recommended using desk lamps, but reluctantly agreed to install light-bulbs between the double layers of glass tubes in his clerestory windows and skylights. The lights were hidden, giving the appearance of natural lighting. He recommended the installation of Aeroshades, commercially available horizontal blinds, on some of the clerestories after workers complained about the glare from the sun.[51]

Wright's building is defined by the Great Workroom, that wonderful open space that explodes with excitement from floor to ceiling by its signature dendriform columns—Matson's building was filled with traditional offices,

The glass tube windows in the Administration Building are beautiful, but they were notorious for leaking.

■   ■   ■

separated by ceilings and walls like every office building of the time. Wright's building was a design unto its own, a streamlined building, that resembled only the sketches Wright had made in 1931 for a proposed newspaper building in Salem, Oregon.[52]

Matson's elevator, like the building itself, was planned as a typical box, but Wright ferried people up and down his three-story building in a pair of circular brass elevators called "bird cages," each four feet in diameter.

The building's signature tall and slender dendriform columns support the weight of the roof. Wright did not want the corners of the building bearing weight, as was the convention at the time. He wrote, "The whole boxing up of human architecture has come to an end."[53]

Columns are often a kind of visual clutter, Lipman says, and Wright could have had fewer columns, if he had used columns with big beams. Instead, he designed "beautiful columns that are slender at their base that in spite of the large number do NOT interrupt the space. . . ."[54] The columns, which measure 18.5 feet in diameter at the top and 9 inches in diameter at the base, were the most dramatic exposition yet of the idea of mushroom-like columns.[55]

Wright's columns took advantage of advances in steel, using steel mesh inside the columns, akin to the structure of the staghorn cactus.[56] The design was so radical that the Wisconsin Industrial Commission refused permission for the building to proceed.[57] Building codes specified a ratio of height to width, according to former Wright apprentice Wes Peters,[58] and the commission did not think that Wright's design would work. Finally it was agreed that a test column would be built on-site.

Tafel remembers the test well. "When it started that morning [June 4, 1937], there was a whole group from Taliesin. They started loading it up with sand and sandbags. They got to 30 tons and there wasn't more room for sand. Wright said get some steel. Ben Wiltscheck [the builder] went to Nash [Nash Motors in Kenosha], and they sent trucks over, and we sent up the steel.

"That's the point when Wright said, 'Edgar, go up the ladder and see if there are any cracks.' I went up the ladder with my camera, and there weren't any cracks. I remember going up that wooden ladder, and that wooden ladder was jiggling the whole time."[59]

The test was a success. Each column needed to support only twelve tons—the test column was loaded with sixty tons, five times what the state required.[60] *The Racine Journal Times* covered the test with four photographs[61]; the caption was headlined "Revolutionizing Architecture."

Wright originally thought of using glass blocks to bring daylight into the building, but eventually turned to Pyrex tubing.[62] The glass tube clerestory windows, one of the building's most notable features, were designed as the building was being built. It was a problem that had yet to be solved when construction started. Wright received seven patents for his design of the aluminum racks that hold the glass tubes, but the tubes were notoriously leaky.

An anonymous construction worker jotted down undated observations about the building on index cards that are filed at Northwestern University: "This is where I worked and watched Wright prove to our building code dept. that this concept was not only functional but safe.

"Pyrex glass were to come up with glass tubing to withstand the heat & cold of changing climates. They failed and great areas had to be covered over with plate glass—also the adhesive used to connect the tubes did not expand & contract with the tubes hence the leaks.

"Beautiful in its concept had technology moved faster to cope with the problems of design. Leaks ruined machines."[63]

Wright also designed the building's famous desks and chairs, which were built by the Metal Office Furniture Company of Grand Rapids, Michigan, the forerunner of Steelcase, Inc. The original chairs had three legs, one in front and two in back. Johnson said in a broadcast interview in 1956 that he often asked Wright why he designed

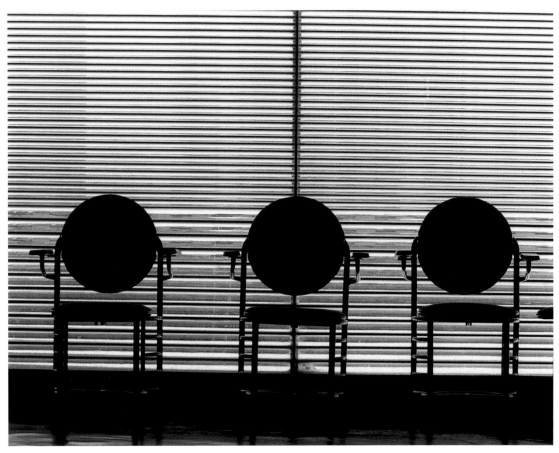

Wright designed the office furniture for the Administration Building.
The chairs shown here have four legs; the originals had only three legs, one in front, two in back.

∎   ∎   ∎

them with three legs, rather than four.[64] "Well, he said that 'you won't tip if you sit back and you put your two feet on the ground because then you've got five legs holding you up. If five legs won't hold you, then I don't know what will.'" Four-legged chairs were commissioned as people began to tip over if they reached for something on the floor.

Steelcase never forgot the importance of the Johnson commission. The company bought the Wright-designed Meyer May house (1908) in Grand Rapids in 1985, and undertook a two-year restoration of the home to its original design as a tribute to Wright.[65] Today those desks and chairs are more than just functional pieces of office furniture, they are also exhibited in such museums as The Art Institute of Chicago, the Metropolitan Museum of Art, and the Milwaukee Art Museum.

Johnson's public relations department was responsible for suggesting the January 1938 issue of *The Architectural Forum*, which was devoted entirely to Wright's work.[66] Lipman says that that issue of the magazine was a "tremendous, powerful vehicle that put Wright in front of the public and virtually inspired a generation of architects that all cited this issue of *Architectural Forum* as having galvanized them." He adds that the magazine was "a reminder that Wright was not buried, but was ahead of all the young folks who were practicing architecture at that time."

Tex Reynolds, the front page columnist of *The Racine Journal Times*, wryly commented on the success of the public open house that helped to inaugurate the building: "No one appreciates architectural beauty more than this writer. But by the time I got out of the jam on Sixteenth Street, I was wishing that Mr. Wright had put up just an ordinary building in which so many folks wouldn't be vitally interested."[67] Crown Prince Frederik and Crown Princess Ingrid of Denmark came to Racine for the four-day celebration.[68] Even local businesses jumped on the bandwagon. Mohr-Jones, a local paint store, took out a full-page ad in the Sunday paper to celebrate the opening of the "modern office building" with "the most spectacular sale of Johnson's Wax Polishes and Paint in History."[69]

Like many of Wright's designs, it is not an easy building to maintain. The company is keenly aware of its responsibility as the steward of such an important Wright work, but that responsibility can be daunting for Ron Wolter, the company's facilities manager. Wolter has to fix a variety of problems, including leaks of one kind or another, as well as face the challenges of modernizing the building to meet twenty-first-century environmental, ergonomic, security, and technological needs. "He [Wright] made a beautiful building," Wolter says. "I wish he could be around here to help once in awhile."[70]

Sam Johnson, the company's chairman emeritus, was 8 years old when H. F. Johnson Jr., his father, took the bold step of embracing the Wright's design proposal in the middle of the Great Depression. It was a decision that has stood the test of time.

Johnson wrote that his father wanted both a building in which the employees "could be happy" as well as a building that would "set us [the company] apart."[71] He has no doubt that Wright succeeded in realizing his father's vision. "Wright is a part of what we are and what we represent. It's part of what we are as a family. It symbolizes our appreciation of art and architecture. Its beauty and creative expression is symbolic of what this company and this family are all about."[72]

"I've hired thousands of people," Johnson says. "I would take them on a tour, and see what's going on in their mind. There's kind of a transformation going on. 'If they have enough guts to build a building like this, which symbolizes the best in contemporary architecture, it must be a company worth working for.'"

Wright's design helped to define the Johnson company. When a Johnson executive asked where the sign would be on the new building, Robert Mosher, a Wright apprentice, replied, "You know the Washington Monument? Well, there's no sign on it."[73]

If the Matson building had been built, it likely would have been just another office building, perhaps one that would have been remodeled several times by now, just like the Hershey building.

Wright had proposed building a $200,000 building that would cost approximately $750,000; it attracted $5 million in publicity the first year it was open, according to H. F. Johnson Jr."[74] The building made Racine a destination for people from around the world who want to tour it, just as Wright predicted.[75] Approximately 4,000 people a year make reservations for the company's weekly architectural tours.

AIRPORT LOUNGE/CAFÉ PROJECT (1941)

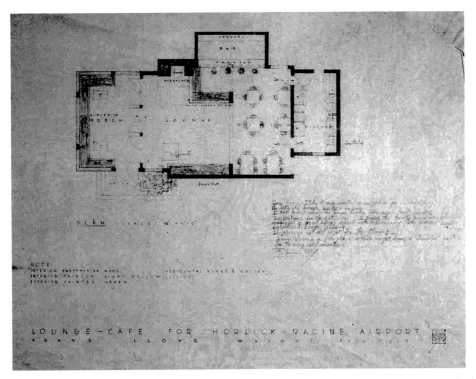

Wright was asked to remodel an existing house on the Horlick Racine Airport property and make it into a lounge and café for the use of the pilots. Johnson chided Wright for including a bar in the plan (rear of the plan); the project was never executed.
© 2004 The Frank Lloyd Wright Foundation
■   ■   ■

Frank Lloyd Wright's smallest—and shortest-lived commission—may have been a proposal in 1941 from H. F. Johnson Jr. and his friend, P. H. Batten, to remodel a house on the property of the Horlick Racine Airport into a pilots' lounge and café in 1941. Batten was president of Twin Disc, another major company in Racine, and president of the airport corporation.

There are only three known letters about the project, two from Johnson to Wright, and one from Wright to Johnson; and a faded copy of a floor plan of Wright's proposal, which has a handwritten note from him to "Hib."[76]

The first letter, from Johnson to Wright, written on June 10, outlines the proposal, for which the airport corporation could budget only $1,000 to $1,500 (equivalent to about $12,000 to $18,000 in 2002).[77] The letter refers to an attached drawing by Batten of the airport site.

The proposal was for an open floor plan, eliminating the walls in the house. Johnson suggested that the interior could have "inexpensive knotty pine wood" paneling because the plaster would probably crack when the house was moved, as planned, from its existing location to a new one. He also proposed a linoleum floor. The porch was to be enclosed in glass.

Batten proposed painting the house a "bright color" and adding a lunch counter. Dotted lines on his drawing showed where a future addition could be built for "ticket office, etc.," according to the letter.

Writing with "Affection," Wright responded on June 14 that he would be happy to make suggestions for the project. "They won't cost you anything but I hope they will be good just the same."

Wright sent his floor plan with the handwritten note to Johnson within days. He wrote that he did not want to make any suggestions for the exterior of the house because he did not know what it looked like. He agreed to Johnson's suggestions for the wood paneling ("waxed with a lemon yellow wax") and linoleum floors, and suggested that the ceiling be replastered.

Johnson wrote back to Wright on June 18 that the airport board would soon study the idea for the lounge/café in detail. He liked the "general idea" of Wright's proposal, although it had too many doors. He had one other criticism: "I am afraid that we will have to eliminate the bar, as that is not such a good thing at an airport." He also wrote "Frank" that a party his daughter had planned had been canceled, but that perhaps Wright could bring his daughter to visit the next time he came to Racine.

It is unknown whether the airport board abandoned the project because of cost, or whether it was derailed by World War II. The answers are lost to history, leaving an unsolved mystery in the quest to know all things Wright.

SC JOHNSON RESEARCH TOWER (1944)

A contorted view of the Research Tower as seen through the tunnel leading to
the Louis Laboratories, the research facility that replaced the Tower in 1982.

■   ■   ■

The lights glow almost until midnight, shimmering through 17.5 miles of Pyrex tube windows, even though the building is now empty. Frank Lloyd Wright's SC Johnson Research Tower opened in 1950, but closed just thirty-two years later, when the company's new research facility, the Louis Laboratories, opened in the former St. Mary's Hospital building across the street.

When H. F. Johnson Jr. and J. V. Steinle, the company's research director, started to plan in 1943 for postwar construction of a new research facility, Johnson was torn between practical considerations and the magnetism of Frank Lloyd Wright and his Administration Building.

Wright initially was told that he would have to bid for the research laboratory commission. Johnson wrote him that while he didn't want to repeat the "financial and construction nightmare" of the Administration Building

The dramatic glass dome was added when the Research Tower was built.
The Johnson Company advertising department was situated under the dome.

The Research Tower is a series of alternating cantilevered square floors (behind the bands of brick) and round mezzanines (behind the glass).

■ ■ ■

Facilities manager Ron Wolter stocks spare Pyrex tubes that can be used, as needed, in the Administration Building and the Research Tower.

■ ■ ■

construction, he felt that Wright should be consulted because the new building would be near his streamlined Administration Building.[78] In 1936 Wright and Johnson had briefly discussed including a tower in the Administration Building complex.[79] Johnson asked Wright for advice about the research building, and suggested that the tower idea be considered.

Johnson avoided Wright's requests to meet with him in person, so Wright wrote him creative and outrageous letters, and then sent him a design for the tower that was ultimately built as the companion piece to his office building.[80] He won the commission, and gave Johnson the landmark tower that a press release likened to a fifteen-story test tube.[81] Today it is difficult to conceive of the sweeping horizontal Administration Building without the tower.

When Wright was a young boy, walking in the woods, he had noticed that trees with tap roots (a single root system) fared better against strong winds than trees with spreading roots. He thought that tall buildings should be like pine trees, with a tap root rather than like elm trees, which have spreading roots.[82] The Research Tower was the first time that Wright was able to build his design for tall buildings, first proposed for the St. Mark's-in-the-Bouwerie project in New York City.

The tower's service core, the tree trunk, sinks fifty-four feet into the ground. The alternating square and round concrete floors are cantilevered from this trunk, like branches. The brick bands of the building delineate the square floors; the mezzanines are shadows visible through the windows between the bands of brick. Construction photographs emphasize the strength of the cantilever, because the core and the floors were built before the exterior walls.

Wright had built numerous homes and a variety of public buildings, but perhaps none had as demanding technical requirements as the research laboratory. It was a highly technical building, but no design detail escaped Wright, which is even more extraordinary considering that he had no computers with which to design his ideas. Facilities manager Ron Wolter admires the work. "He just didn't do it easy, and it all fits." He marvels at the accents in the building. "Why would anyone have done that? That's what's fun about it."[83]

The Research Tower was tuck-pointed in 2001, as part of the company's commitment to maintain the building, which has been empty since 1982. The mortar joints between the bricks were finished with a narrow ridge of mortar.

■   ■   ■

There are nooks and crannies in the tower. There are variations in the shape of the handrails on the stairs. In a subtle detail that perhaps says the most about Wright's work, in some areas there is a course of bricks just below

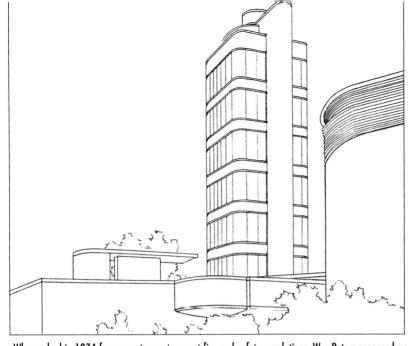

When asked in 1974 for a way to meet current fire and safety regulations, Wes Peters proposed an external stairwell for the south side of the Research Tower, as shown in this plan.

© 2004 The Frank Lloyd Wright Foundation, used with permission of SC Johnson. ▪ ▪ ▪

the mezzanine, which gradually tapers down to about ⅛ inch. How the masons must have cursed Wright!

"It could have been worse, though," says Wolter, pointing to Wright's original design, which called for a tapered tower wider at the top than at the bottom. Such a design would have meant that every course of brick and every band of glass tube windows be a different size than the one above and below it. Wright had first proposed a tapered design for St. Mark's, reasoning that the building would stay cleaner because rain would not drip onto the floor below (he also thought that the upper floors could garner higher rents because they were wider).[84]

Safety concerns were a large part of the decision to move out of the tower into the former hospital building across the street in 1982. Wright had originally proposed two small elevators and two staircases for the tower.[85] J. V. Steinle thought that one larger elevator to carry freight was needed, and only one elevator and one narrow staircase (with steps measuring only up to 29.5 inches across) were in the finished building.

Wright had refused to allow a sprinkler system for aesthetic reasons.[86] It would have been impossible to get a fire ladder truck into the tower courtyard under the low roof of the surrounding enclosure. Experiments using combustibles could not be conducted in the tower.

Questions about the employees' ability to quickly evacuate the building in an emergency prompted then-president Sam Johnson to commission Taliesin Associated Architects to design a new, code-compliant fire escape system in 1974. Wes Peters' solution, probably the only one possible, was to add a new stairwell to the exterior of the south side of the tower. Looking at that design almost thirty years later, Johnson writes, "I guess this is one . . . project that I'm glad we passed on, particularly when I discovered that very few of our scientists really wanted to stay there."[87]

Complaints from scientists who worked in the building included glare when the sun was shining, lack of light after sundown, lack of a view through the glass tube windows, and difficulties heating and cooling the building.[88]

There was extensive discussion during the 1970s about how to accommodate the company's changing research needs and how to adapt the tower to different uses. One proposal was an expansion of the research facilities north from the tower.[89] At various times the company also discussed plans for a company library or a think tank in the tower.[90] Johnson says that he declined to implement a suggestion that he move his office into the tower because a tower office, far removed from everyone else, would not fit his management style.

Some say that the building was a practical failure. Johnson acknowledges that the building "didn't work as well as Wright envisioned, because he didn't understand how scientists work together."[91] He contrasts the open space of the Great Workroom in the Administration Building with the

Some scientists enjoyed working in the relative isolation of the Research Tower, which is in stark contrast to the wide open Great Workroom of the Administration Building.

■   ■   ■

layout of the tower, noting the "inconvenience of going into an elevator" to consult with colleagues in a building that had no conference rooms or long hallways.

Still, some scientists did enjoy working in the tower. Fred Billman, who worked there from 1969 to 1974, enjoyed the relative isolation,[92] finding it conducive to productivity. He also remembers lighter moments, when workers on the square floors would float balloons to their colleagues on the mezzanine above.

"In many ways it was a functioning failure, but it was a spiritual success," Johnson says as he reflects on the building's legacy.[93] He emphatically disputes the notion that the building was a complete failure. Proof of this is

Johnson Company's Wright campus is marked by dramatic shapes; it has come to symbolize the creative spirit of the organization.

■   ■   ■

threefold, he says, mentioning Raid, Pledge, and Edge, the company's most successful brands. "They all got hatched up when the tower was there. Who's to say that wasn't the Wright influence?"

It is warm and a bit stuffy as one walks through each empty floor on a hot summer day, twenty years after the researchers moved across the street, but the building is in remarkable condition. Some deserted buildings are eerie; this one is not. There is a sense that someone could walk back in, do a bit of fix-up work, and the building would come alive again. Black stone countertops on the lab benches are empty. Some are square; some are curved, depending on the workspace. They sit atop metal drawers and cabinets of every shape imaginable. Some cabinets are painted brown, some beige, some green; others are Wright's famed Cherokee red. Some are still labeled "Jar covers 4 oz." Countless chrome faucets and nozzles abound. Miles of pipes run under the Cherokee red floor tiles; several have brass handles on them, so that they can be serviced.

Johnson says that there is no question about maintaining the building. "Its beauty and creative expression is symbolic of what this company and this family are all about." Wright, he adds, "is a part of what we are and what we represent. He stood up for what he believed in, and championed new ideas and free expression." As for the maintenance costs, "No one likes the maintenance costs. [But] It's like protecting your home ground. If you outgrow it, which we've done, it's still our roots, our symbol."[94]

In 2001, the company cleaned those 17.5 miles of windows (with the company's Windex Outdoor, of course) and repaired damaged brickwork. Workers traveled up and down the sides of the Tower on a motorized scaffold in the evening and at night all summer, when the company campus was almost deserted. They had a spectacular view of the city and Lake Michigan as the sun set. They looked like eerie creatures when viewed through the building's glass tube walls. The tower may never reopen, but it stands—literally and figuratively—as a beacon for the company. "It's still an architectural gem," says Sam Johnson, although he doesn't know what the future holds for the building.[95] "I'll leave it to the next generation to figure out what to do with the tower."

In 1947, H. F. Johnson Jr. asked Wright how the company could add more office space in the future.[96] Four years later, in 1951, Wright drew plans for a two-story office addition that could be built on top of the carport on the east side of the tower. Being Frank Lloyd Wright, he didn't simply add two stories of conventional office; he proposed a two-story light well that would run through the center of the addition. John Halama, the company architect, modified the plans with Wright's approval in 1957. Construction began in 1960—a year after Wright died—and was completed in 1961. Wes Peters of Taliesin Associated architects, the successor firm to Wright, drew the final plans. The light well was eliminated to add even more needed office space, which was very much needed.

YWCA (1949, 1950)

America was filled with postwar optimism in 1946 when Racine's YWCA bought land for a new building at 740 College Avenue, across from the fourteen-story Racine County Courthouse. H. F. Johnson Jr. retained Wright in May 1949, but two other architects competed for the commission. John Batten, another Racine business leader, preferred local architect Frank Hoffman. Fitzhugh Scott Jr., who had designed the Milwaukee YWCA, also submitted plans, and was ultimately hired.

Scott's building, which opened in 1953, is streamlined, with a round corner and a circular, glass-lined stair tower at the southeast end. Visitors find themselves in a typical lobby and reception area. A variety of doors lead to the pool, locker rooms, a meeting room, and the stairs. It has served the community well for fifty years, but it is not the ambitious, bold, and exciting building that Wright had proposed.

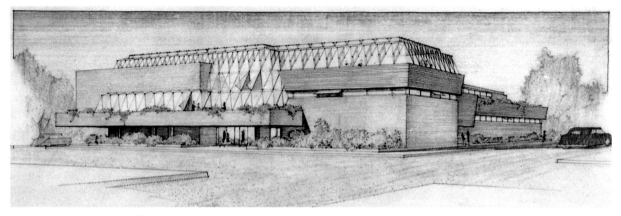

Wright proposed to build a dramatic building, with a swimming pool under a glass roof.
Courtesy Racine Heritage Museum Collections, © 2004 The Frank Lloyd Wright Foundation

■   ■   ■

Wright's plans for the Y—like many of his public buildings—brought in natural light to celebrate the interior.[97] Few holes were punched into the sides of the building to serve as traditional windows; instead, there were clerestory windows, a style that Wright often used, and a dramatic glass canopy over the entrance, a glass waterfall cascading down from a glass roof. They illuminated the open lobby and a rooftop swimming pool. The roof was really the crowning touch.

Visitors would have entered into a large, open reception area. There was no low ceiling to compress space. Wright's lobby was an atrium that flowed up into the glass roof, allowing the entire building to breathe. His lobby led to three floors connected by ramps, with tropical plants, under the skylight roof. Plans included an activity room for teenagers, music and crafts rooms, bowling alleys, and a gymnasium.

Wright drew two sets of plans for the project, the first in 1949 and the second in 1950. The builder would have been Ben Wiltscheck, who had worked with Wright on the Johnson Administration Building and Research Tower, and on Wingspread. Two letters from Wright to the Y explain why his building was not built.[98]

On January 30, 1950, Wright sent a pleasant letter to Barbara Sargent, secretary of the Building Committee. He wrote that his revised plans included "all the changes except the solid roof." He explained the kind of roof he wanted. "I had hoped for a translucent overhead, sloped so that it would require cleaning but twice a year—no danger of leaks in this over-lapping form of glass-slab technique."

Then he addressed the cost of the building. "I have had as my goal in this case a straight-forward building costing within $500,000.00 and believe it can be built for that sum without difficulty." Furniture, except for built-ins, was not included in the estimate.

The lobby of the YWCA was to include an airy atrium, with concrete ramps.

■   ■   ■

He chided Sargent not to be guided by the "wholly irresponsible" cost estimates from "so-called outside experts" who wouldn't be familiar with his building techniques. Perhaps he hoped that committee members didn't know his reputation for going over budget, assuring her, "In the light of my previous experience—it is considerable—I think you have no reason to fear much, if any, increase over the half-million as mentioned."

All that was needed, Wright concluded, was a note from the board to Johnson, approving the plans and a request for him to make presumably more detailed plans, "a tedious clerical business requiring some time." It would be worth it. "I think we are going to have a remarkably fine and useful structure; one to be proud of and one the Y.W.C.A. does need as a sign of cultural vitality no matter how self-satisfied it may be."

Wright resigned the commission six weeks later, in a terse note dated March 17: "My dear Ladies: Concerning the work I have done in your behalf by generosity of Mr. Herbert Johnson, there seems to be some mistake. Mr. Wiltscheck . . . tells me you have been deliberating between these drawings submitted by me and those of other architects. This deliberation places me in a position I have never accepted knowingly and never shall. I do not compete for work." He concluded, "So, reluctantly, I withdraw my services at this point hoping that what I have done may be of some benefit to you and whatever architects you see fit to employ. As for architects willing to work under such circumstances I have nothing but contempt— which is shared by their own American Institute of Architects."

The correspondence between Johnson and Wright is more revealing. It is poignant and intimate.[99] On December 20, 1949, Wright wrote to Johnson, frustrated that "owing to some Milwaukee fool's estimate" of the cost of the building, the Y board was "worried about cost." Then, after mocking the Y for worrying about costs, he ends the letter with a possible admission of financial imprudence: "So please Hib—you are worthy of your hire—the laborer is worthy of his. . . . The sum now due is $15,000.00—already all spent—but we won't let you down. . . . We never have. We never will. Affection."

A month later, on January 23, Wright wrote: "Dear Hib: Don't 'worry'—it doesn't become you. You have a lot on the ball—come hell, come high water. You can only lose by worry. Tentative baby-check (and sketches) came finally from the Y.W.C.A. We find it quite feasible to make the changes they wanted. In the main they seem very happy and proud of the prospect of having such a building. We will see the whole thing stays simple and straight forward building throughout. Trouble here is we ended the year about $16,000.00 in the red so far as we know anything. Pulling a pretty heavy load toward the end of the line? You have been pretty good to me, Hib, on the whole, within your lights. You could not have been better to your own father. I have an idea he would approve your relationship to me. But, how do I know?"

Johnson acknowledged the end of Wright's commission on April 11: "Dear Frank: It looks like the whole deal on the YWCA has been called off—so I owe $7,500, which I am enclosing. I look forward to seeing you this summer. . . ."

Five decades later, Johnson's son, Sam Johnson, recalls the project. "He [H. F. Johnson Jr.] was really irritated that they didn't think twice about having Wright do the building."[100]

Bruce Brooks Pfeiffer characterized the Y proposal as "a remarkably detailed and thought-out scheme that could serve as a community center for any smaller American city."[101] When the Racine Heritage Museum was looking at designs for a new building early in 2003, the board asked former Wright apprentice Charles Montooth of Taliesin Architects to see if Wright's YWCA plan could be adapted. The cost was prohibitive, and the museum board chose another design.[102] Renderings of Wright's YWCA are displayed at the museum, but the building itself remains unbuilt.

There is a perception that Frank Lloyd Wright built houses only for wealthy people. On the contrary, Wright was very concerned with the need for quality homes for the middle class.[1] Robert P. Harrison observed that "Wright conceived of housing as the basis of American democracy, not as the privilege of the rich."[2] He manifested this concern in the development of the Usonian house model during the early 1930s, and in designs for several planned housing communities, some never constructed. Wright had a connection to two planned housing communities in Racine that were contemplated but never built: the Monolith Homes[3] and the Johnson Homes.

Rudolph Schindler, who designed the Monolith Homes, erased Wright's names from some of the drawings. Schindler accused Wright of taking credit for his work.

From the Monolith Homes Project Files, R. M. Schindler archive, Architecture and Design Collection, University Art Museum at the University of California, Santa Barbara, and used with permission.

■ ■ ■

THE MONOLITH HOMES (1919)

Wright is better known for the private homes he designed, but he also wanted to design an economical, mass-produced housing system.[4] The Monolith Homes, commissioned by Thomas P. Hardy, Wright's first Racine client, evolved from the American System-Built houses, built for Arthur Richards in Milwaukee (1916).[5]

The commission is listed in the official Wright project database (PR#1901). A patent for the concrete engineering was issued August 18, 1919,[6] and Wright signed off on at least several of the plans, but the design itself was not his.[7] The Monolith Homes were actually designed by Rudolph Schindler in Wright's Chicago office while Wright was in Tokyo working on the Imperial Hotel. Wright and Schindler had a bitter falling out in 1931 when Schindler accused Wright of trying to take undue credit for Schindler's work on a variety of commissions, including the Monolith Homes.[8]

A colony of eighteen workers' homes would be built from one set of concrete forms.
© 2004 The Frank Lloyd Wright Foundation

■   ■   ■

There are two identical perspective drawings of the Monolith Homes, one in the Frank Lloyd Wright Foundation archives and the other in the R. M. Schindler archives at the University Art Museum at the University of California, Santa Barbara. The first drawing shows "Frank Lloyd Wright Architect" above Schindler's signature. Wright's name has been erased from the one in the Schindler archives. As their dispute intensified, Schindler very possibly erased Wright's name on the drawing that Schindler still owned.

A workers' community of eighteen concrete buildings was to have been built on West High Street, near today's Colonial Park, across the Root River from where the Keland house was built in 1954. The layout was staggered, to avoid the appearance of city row houses, and plans called for a community laundry in the first house.[9]

Only one set of forms was to be made for the floors and outside walls of all eighteen buildings.[10] Inside walls would have two coats of plaster. Kitchen counters would be maple; all exposed woodwork would be of first-quality cypress, with two coats of oil stain. The concept was "one entire structure of poured concrete, strong, vermin-proof, fireproof."[11] Vertical strips of glass, sometimes one story high, sometimes two stories high, were part of the design as well.[12] The living room had inverted corner windows, formed by two adjoining vertical pieces of glass.[13] The floor plan was a cruciform, with a living room, two-story dining room, and kitchen on the first floor, and two bedrooms and two porches (including an outdoor sleeping porch) on the second floor.[14]

By the spring of 1920, the name of the community was changed to Monolith Residences, and the idea of a concrete building was abandoned in favor of a concrete foundation and a stucco and wood frame construction, like the Richards Duplex Apartments in Milwaukee.[15]

Scholar Kathryn Smith has extensively researched Schindler's work. She has traced the design evolution of Schindler's Monolith Homes through aspects of Wright's design of the concrete textile block Storer (1923) and Freeman (1923–1924) houses in California, through the unbuilt Chandler Block House (1927) to the full-length corner window design at Fallingwater.[16] It is not known why the project was not executed.

THE JOHNSON HOMES (1948)

Wright originally envisioned an entire Johnson community for the SC Johnson Administration Building. H. F. Johnson Jr. rejected the concept in 1936, but in 1948 he explored the idea of helping employees obtain mortgages for 200 to 400 Wright-designed homes to be built in the area now known as Wind Meadows, southwest of Wingspread.[17] Johnson was concerned about the company's employees, but he also wanted to ensure that an outside developer did not build an unwelcome development around Wingspread.[18]

In 1982, Jonathan Lipman interviewed a real estate developer who told him that Johnson was unable to raise the money for the project from real estate equity firms.[19] Johnson's son, Sam, recalls that his father rejected the plan because it "used up too much land for too little benefit."[20] The family ultimately worked with another developer to build and sell homes, not just for employees, in Wind Meadows.[21] In a recent conversation I had with Karen Boyd Johnson, she wondered if her father may have also considered using the land he and friends owned west of the Root River—toward what is now Valley View Drive—where she built her home in 1954, for this project.

No records of any proposed designs by Wright exist, but Lipman has no doubt about what the project would have meant. He writes that the Johnson Homes—as he calls them—"would have been by a factor of ten the largest collection of houses designed by Wright. They would have made Racine a cultural tourism site of great note. They would have made Wright's position in the public's eye, and his reputation among architects, and his prominence in national shelter magazines, much greater even than it was."[22]

APPENDIX A

Following is the text of the letter that Frank Lloyd Wright wrote to H. F. Johnson Jr., trying to persuade Johnson to award him the commission to design the company's new research facility. The letter is dated December 14, 1943.

Dear Hibbard:

It hath reached me, O King of the Age, that Aladdin said to the sultan, "Why build a heavy building sodden upon the ground facing awkwardly upon unsightly streets when, by creating a charming interior space for parking, the lighting would come from above or from the court? A gallery would follow above and around the court space, O Master, and bridge tunnels would be seen connecting this space and the administration building itself to the research laboratory which has a tall shaft that would rise from the center of the court, etc., my lord, etc. Thy subjects would like to traverse the bridge tunnels even similar to the one thou now hast, etc., etc., from which to look down upon a goodly garden from the center of the spacious parking and, O Kelif, why not broadcast the year round your good tidings and amusing, too, from the top of the 18 stories from an inexpensive but beautiful radio mast rising out of the utmost height. And should not thy research extend to packaging containers, etc., etc., etc., and define a complete little printing plant where brochures by thy worthy self such as thou hast sent me to read could be executed? What a miracle of beautiful planning will be there to instruct thy foes, delight thy friends and convince thy subjects of the illustrious character of they reign, O my Kelif, and in all arguments as to thy power, excellence, and majesty. Affection, Frank Lloyd Wright

Listed by year, project record number from the Frank Lloyd Wright Archives, and address.

1901 PR#0117: Miles house, proposal to remodel 2300 Washington Ave. (unbuilt)

1905 PR#0506: Hardy house, 1319 Main St.

1919 PR#1901: Monolith Homes, W. High St., near Colonial Park (unbuilt)

1936 PR#3601: SC Johnson Administration Building, 1525 Howe St.

1937 PR#3703: H. F. Johnson Jr. house (Wingspread), 33 E. Four Mile Road

1938 PR#3808, 3815: Wingspread gatehouse and farm (unbuilt)

1941 PR#4116: Roy Petersen house, originally designed for Edith Carlson (1939), built in Ann Arbor in 1979 as the Whitford-Haddock house

1941 PR#4117: Racine-Horlick Airport lounge/café, 3239 N. Green Bay Road (unbuilt)

1944 PR#4401: SC Johnson Research Tower, 1515 Howe St.

1949 PR#4920: YWCA, 740 College Ave. (unbuilt)

1950 PR#5041: YWCA, 740 College Ave. (unbuilt)

1951 PR#5124: Addition to SC Johnson office space surrounding Research Tower

1954 PR#5517: Karen Johnson Keland house, 1425 Valley View Drive

The public side of the Keland house is understated. Its drama is in the courtyard and on the river side of the house.

■ ■ ■

Frank Lloyd Wright's influence on Racine architecture goes beyond his own work, through the work of former apprentices and associates. (Donald Rintz, *Frank Lloyd Wright and Prairie School Architecture: Tour Guide* Racine: Racine Landmarks Preservation Commission, 1994—includes photographs and details about these commissions).

FRANCIS BARRY BYRNE was an apprentice in Wright's studio in Oak Park from 1902 to 1907 and worked in the studio until 1908. He worked on drawings for the Unity Temple and Meeting House in Oak Park, Illinois (1905) and the Coonley house in Riverside, Illinois (1907). He designed three buildings in Racine:

- St. Catherine's High School (1923), 1200 Park Ave.
- St. Patrick's Catholic Church (1924), 1100 Erie St.
- St. Patrick's School (1924), 1109 Douglas Ave.

EDGAR TAFEL was an apprentice in the Taliesin Fellowship from 1932 to 1941. He supervised construction of the SC Johnson Administration Building and of Wingspread, as well as part of Fallingwater. A dispute with Wright over his first commission, the Albert House, led to Tafel's decision to leave the Fellowship. He designed six homes in Racine:

- Albert House (1940), Village of North Bay, not visible from the street.
- Gottlieb House (1946), 432 Wolff St.
- Silver House (1947), 2910 Michigan Blvd. (an addition from the 1970s hides some of the original design).
- Nelsen House (1947), 2536 Green Haze Ave.
- Louis Hamilton House (1949), 4001 Haven Ave.
- Robert Hamilton House (1949), 5345 Wind Point Road.

CHARLES MONTOOTH began his apprenticeship at Taliesin in 1945. He was a member of Taliesin Associated Architects after Wright's death in 1959, until the firm was restructured in 2003.

- Prairie School (1965, and all additions), 4959 Lighthouse Drive.
- Whitford-Haddock house [1979, Ann Arbor, Michigan, from the plans for the unbuilt Roy Petersen house (1939)].

ALPHONSO IANNELLI was a sculptor who worked with Wright on the Midway Gardens (1913) in Chicago. He worked with Byrne on St. Catherine's High School and St. Patrick's Church.

JENS JENSEN, who landscaped Wright's Coonley house and Roberts house in Marquette, Michigan (1936), designed Island Park, Riverside Park, and Washington Park in Racine, and made plans for other projects in Racine, including Monument Square, which were not executed.

TOURS

SC Johnson Administration Building
1525 Howe St.
Enter from 14th and Franklin
Guided tours are offered by reservation
    only: 262.260.2154.

Wingspread, 33 East Four Mile Road
Guided tours are offered by reservation
    only: 262.681.3353
Fax 262.681.3960
tour@johnsonfdn.org

PERMANENT MUSEUM EXHIBIT

Racine Heritage Museum
701 Main Street
262.636.3926
www.spiritofinnovation.org

GENERAL INFORMATION

Preservation Racine
P.O. Box 393
Racine, WI 53401
262.634.5749
info@preservationracine.org
www.preservationracine.org

Racine County Convention and Visitors Bureau
14015 Washington Ave.
Sturtevant, WI 53177
1-800.2.RACINE
www.visitracine.org

Frank Lloyd Wright® Wisconsin Heritage Program
P.O. Box 6339
Madison, WI 53716-0339
608.287.0339
www.wrightinwiscsonsin.org

Preface

1. Taliesin Preservation, Inc., *The Love of an Idea*, fund-raising brochure. Spring Green, WI: Taliesin Preservation, 1999, p. 2. Donald Hoffmann discussed the relationship between Wright's building and nature in *Frank Lloyd Wright: Architecture and Nature*. New York: Dover, 1986.

2. Samuel C. Johnson, *The Essence of a Family Enterprise*. Racine: S. C. Johnson & Son, Inc., 1988, p. 137. The remark was made September 15, 1951, in a talk to the Taliesin Fellowship.

3. Edgar Tafel, *Frank Lloyd Wright: Recollections by Those Who Knew Him*. New York: Dover, 1993. I particularly recommend this book for its variety of essays about Wright by people who knew him.

4. John Buenker and Richard Ammann, *Invention City: The Sesquicentennial History of Racine*. Racine: Racine Heritage Museum, 1998, p. iv.

5. Descriptions of inventions from Buenker and Ammann, and Jim Kneiszel, "Belle City Ingenuity," in *Celebrate Racine: A Look at a Unique Community,* The Journal Times, 1997, pp. 73–77.

6. "The Story of Johnson Wax," press release and visitors information, undated, the 1980s. The company was later known as S. C. Johnson & Son, Inc., Johnson Wax, and SC Johnson Wax, but today it is known as SC Johnson, which is the reference used throughout this book.

7. Wright's Prairie home designs broke down the rigid, formal interiors of conventional residential architecture. They opened up to the landscape, and featured open interior spaces that flowed into each other rather than traditional, distinct rooms separated by walls. Wright custom designed his window, lighting, and furniture designs to be highly integrated into the design of each house.

8. Anthony Alofsin, *Frank Lloyd Wright: The Lost Years, 1910–1922*. Chicago: University of Chicago Press, 1993, p. 372, fn. 28.

9. Olgivanna Wright, quoted by Jonathan Lipman, *Frank Lloyd Wright and the Johnson Wax Buildings*. New York: Rizzoli, 1986, p. 39.

10. Wright's Usonian designs were generally for modest and moderately priced homes, with open floor plans and small bedrooms. A generous "great room" that combined the dining, living, and family rooms and opened to the site made the relatively small houses feel remarkably expansive.

11. Wright likened the core of the building to a tree trunk, from which the floors were cantilevered like branches. St. Mark's was never built, apparently because of the Stock Market crash.

12. Letter from Wright to the YWCA, March 17, 1950, courtesy Racine Heritage Museum Collections.

13. Edgar Tafel, interview with the author, August 16, 2003. Tafel's reference is to the Taliesin Fellowship that Wright started in 1932, when he lacked work and was experiencing great financial difficulties.

14. Johnson, interview with the author, August 27, 2001.

Chapter 1

1. Frank Lloyd Wright, *An Autobiography: Frank Lloyd Wright*. New York: Longmans, 1932, p. 67.

2. The Mitchell house was designed the year after Wright left Adler and Sullivan, when Wright no longer had to hide his work in Corwin's name. Corwin is listed as the architect in the March 1894 *Inland Architect and News Record,* just two lines above a listing of one of Wright's own works, the Bagley house in Hinsdale, IL. The theory that Wright was the architect is based on conjecture; no facts support the idea.

3. OsKär Muñoz, Frank Lloyd Wright Foundation, e-mail to the author, October 20, 2003, after the author had submitted documentation of the project. The Miles house project is now listed as PR#0117. The story of the Miles house commission was first published in a copyright article by the author in Racine's *The Journal Times,* November 2, 2003.

4. Corwin's and Wright's letters and designs are used with permission of the McCormick Library of Special Collections, Northwestern University Library.

5. Wright and Corwin had shared office space, but were never partners.

6. Wright also used a pinwheel design in Racine in 1937 when he designed Wingspread.

7. Robert Hartmann, interview with the author, October 29, 2003.

8. Jean Harris, interviews with the author, October 30 and November 20, 2003.

9. Many of the houses are shown in Susan E. Karr, *Architectural and Historical Survey of the City of Racine*. Racine: Racine Landmarks Preservation Commission, 1980, and Donald Rintz, *Southside Historic District Walking Tour Guide*. Racine: Racine Landmarks Preservation Commission, 1993.

10. Wright, p. 123.

11. C. E. Percival, "A House on a Bluff," *House Beautiful,* June 1906, reproduced in Diane Maddex, *Frank Lloyd Wright's House Beautiful.* New York: Hearst Books, 2000, p. 29.

12. Jonathan Lipman, *Frank Lloyd Wright and the Johnson Wax Buildings.* New York: Rizzoli, 1986, p. 13.

13. Wright, p. 138.

14. Anne Sporer Ruetz, interview with the author, September 9, 2003.

15. Robert McCarter, *Frank Lloyd Wright.* London: Phaidon Press, 1997, p. 90.

16. Ruetz, interview, September 9, 2003.

17. Ruetz, interview, September 25, 2003.

18. Ruetz, e-mail to the author, September 23, 2003.

19. John J. McCusker, "Comparing the Purchasing Power of Money in the United States (or Colonies) from 1665–2002," *Economic History Services,* 2003; http://www.eh.net/hmit/ppowerusd/.

20. Copy of Bill of Sale given to the author by Anne Sporer Ruetz.

21. Letter from Thomas P. Hardy to Wright, June 15, 1936, © 2004 The Frank Lloyd Wright Foundation.

22. 1941 plans owned by the current homeowner, viewed by the author, September 9, 2003.

23. Percival, in Maddex, p. 29.

24. Herbert Jacobs, *Frank Lloyd Wright: America's Greatest Architect.* New York: Harcourt, Brace & World, 1965, p. 126.

25. Donna Newgord, tour coordinator, interview with the author, October 24, 2003.

26. Prairie Architects, *Wingspread Historical Structures Report.* Fairfield, IA: Prairie Architects, Inc., 1995, p. IV-11.

27. Ibid., Fig. IV-13.

28. *The Architectural Forum,* January 1938, p. 56. The entire issue was devoted to Wright's work.

29. Prairie Architects, p. IV-14.

30. Measurements in this and the following paragraphs are from the brochure *Wingspread,* The Johnson Foundation, Inc., 1996.

31. David A. Hanks, *The Decorative Designs of Frank Lloyd Wright.* New York: Dutton, 1979, p. 152.

32. Edgar Tafel, interview with the author, October 24, 2003.

33. Jonathan Lipman, interview with the author, April 14, 2003, and e-mail from Lipman to the author, October 17, 2003.

34. Karen Johnson Boyd, interview with the author, June 26, 2003.

35. Prairie Architects, p. IV-36.

36. Ibid., p. IV-34.

37. Boyd, interview, June 26, 2003.

38. Prairie Architects, p. IV-36.

39. Tafel, interview, May 15, 2003.

40. Prairie Architects, p. IV-77.

41. Tafel, interview, July 23, 2003.

42. Samuel C. Johnson, "Mr. Wright and the Johnsons of Racine, Wis.", *AIA Journal,* January 1979, p. 3.

43. Samuel C. Johnson, interview with the author, March 31, 2003.

44. Boyd, interview, June 26, 2003.

45. Prairie Architects, p. IV-43.

46. Boyd, interview, September 29, 2003.

47. Prairie Architects, p. IV-85.

48. Ibid., p. IV-86 and Fig. IV-90.

49. Ibid., p. IV-47.

50. Johnson, *AIA Journal*, p. 4.

51. Robin Langley Sommer, *Frank Lloyd Wright: A Gatefold Portfolio*. New York: Barnes & Noble, 1997.

52. Bruce Brooks Pfeiffer, *Frank Lloyd Wright Monograph 1936–1941*, vol. 6, edited and photographed by Yukio Futagawa. Tokyo: A.D.A. Edita, 1986, p. 202.

53. Ibid., p. 298. Wright's Broadacre City vision was for society to embrace a very low-density, "non-urban" development, with far less emphasis on cities as the central focus of economic and social life. In his *Autobiography* (1932), Wright predicted the growth of chain stores, the demise of railroads as networks of highway spread, and the concept of an expanded gas station as a social center for communities.

54. Boyd, interview, June 26, 2003.

55. Boyd, interview, September 29, 2003.

56. Lipman, e-mail to the author, October 2, 2003.

57. Boyd, interview, September 29, 2003.

58. Ibid.

59. Comments during "Working with Wright . . . An Evening of Conversation with Clients" (panel discussion), Milwaukee Art Museum, October 2, 3003, and Boyd, interview, November 25, 2003.

60. Boyd, interview, September 29, 2003.

61. Ibid.

62. Boyd, interview, June 26, 2003.

63. Wright, p. 142.

64. Boyd, interview, November 17, 2003.

65. Boyd, interview, September 29, 2003.

66. Bill Keland, interview with the author, October 5, 2003.

67. Comments during "Working with Wright . . . An Evening of Conversation with Clients."

68. Bill Boyd at his home, conversation with the author, October 31, 2002.

69. Karen Johnson Boyd, interview with the author for *Wright in Racine*, video production to accompany permanent exhibit at the Racine Heritage Museum, © 2001 by RHM, Inc.

Chapter 2

1. Matson created a large body of public architecture in Racine, including City Hall, the church that is now the George Bray Neighborhood Center, Horlick and Park high schools, and Mitchell School.

2. Jonathan Lipman, *Frank Lloyd Wright and the Johnson Wax Buildings*. New York: Rizzoli, 1986, p. 9. This is the definitive book on the subject.

3. Blueprints viewed by the author, April 9, 2002.

4. Edgar Tafel, interview with the author, December 12, 2001.

5. Mattie Newell, Matson's sister, interview with the author, January 14, 2002; she recalls Matson going to Hershey.

6. Lipman, p. 1.

7. Ibid.

8. Edgar Tafel, *Years with Frank Lloyd Wright*. New York: Dover, 1979, p. 175.

9. Lipman, p. 1.

10. Tafel.

11. Serge Logan, interviews with the author, February 6, 2002 and September 14, 2003.

12. Frank Lloyd Wright, *An Autobiography: Frank Lloyd Wright*. New York: Horizon Press, 1977, p. 494.

13. Lipman, p. 3.

14. Tafel, interview, December 12, 2001. He was not at the meeting, but he recounted what he had been told.

15. E.O. Jim Jones, Johnson public relations director who retired in 1980, interview with the author, October 23, 2003, recounting conversations with E. Willis Jones.

16. Letter from Jack Ramsey to H. F. Johnson Jr., July 19, 1936.

17. Ramsey letter, p.1, typed transcript of handwritten letter.

18. Olgivanna Lloyd Wright, *Frank Lloyd Wright: His Life, His Work, His Words*. New York: Horizon Press, 1966, p. 130.

19. Wright, p. 494. In a September 11, 2003, e-mail to the author, Jonathan Lipman wrote that the retainer was $1,000.

20. Ramsey letter transcript, p. 1.

21. Ibid., p. 2.

22. Ibid.

23. Ibid., p. 3.

24. Ibid., p. 1.

25. Ibid., p. 5.

26. Stuart Macaulay, e-mail to the author, October 24, 2003. Macaulay, professor of contract law at the University of Wisconsin, wrote an interesting perspective about the legal implications of the Johnson building being built without a formal contract, "Organic Transactions: Contract, Frank Lloyd Wright and the Johnson Building," *Wisconsin Law Review,* 1996, no. 1.

27. Lipman, p. 13.

28. Lipmann, e-mail to the author, February 3, 2002.

29. Lipman, p. 13.

30. Wright, p. 499. There are many parallels among the stories of the Larkin and the Johnson buildings. Apprentice Wesley Peters wrote about them in a May 5, 1937, newspaper column in Randolph C. Henning's *At Taliesin,* a collection of newspaper columns by Wright and the apprentices. They are also apparent in Brendan Gill's discussion of the Larkin building in *Many Masks,* his biography of Wright. Ramsey's letter to H. F. Johnson Jr. is reminiscent of W. E. Martin's letter to his brother, Darwin, October 2, 1902, in which he was effusive in his praise of Wright and hoped that John Larkin would recognize Wright's genius. The Larkins' opinion that the building would bring in favorable publicity that would far outweigh the cost overruns has a parallel to the Johnson building as well.

31. Ibid.

32. Patrick J. Meehan, *The Master Architect: Conversations with Frank Lloyd Wright*. New York: Wiley, 1984, p. 16.

33. Karen Johnson Boyd, interviews with the author, February 12, 2002 and June 6, 2003.

34. Lipman, p. 13.

35. Tafel, interview, December 12, 2001.

36. Ibid.

37. Ibid. Tafel said that Wright often drew out the end of his name. Wright wrote in his *Autobiography* that he was driven to Racine 132 times as the building was being planned and constructed. The distance is about 330 miles round trip on today's roads. Part of Highway 14, between Spring Green (where Taliesin is located) and Middleton, on Madison's west side, is now called the Frank Lloyd Wright Memorial Highway.

38. Tafel, interview, December 12, 2001.

39. Ibid.

40. Tafel, interview, August 16, 2003.

41. Ibid.

42. Lipman, p. 32.

43. Ibid., p.15.

44. Ibid., p. 31.

45. Ibid.

46. "Johnson's (sic) Building New Office," *The Racine Journal Times,* December 31, 1936.

47. A similar description is included in a lengthy statement Wright wrote on October 11, 1936, at the company's request for a press release; the entire text is in Lipman, pp.182–183.

48. Lipman, e-mail, September 12, 2003.

49. Ibid.

50. Lipman, p. 68.

51. Ibid., p. 93.

52. Wright, p. 495; renderings of the building are in Lipman, pp. 8, 10, 11.

53. Olgivanna Lloyd Wright, p.156.

54. Lipman, e-mail, September 11, 2003. (Emphasis in original.)

55. C. A. P. Turner used less dramatic mushroom columns in the Johnson-Bovey Building in Minneapolis (1905–1906), as did Robert Maillart's Zurcher Lagerhaus-Gesellschaft Warehouse in Zurich-Glesshubel, Switzerland (1910). Wright used small mushroom columns in his A. D. German Warehouse in Richland Center (1915).

56. Lipman, p. 56.

57. Ibid., p. 59.

58. Lipman, e-mail, September 11, 2003.

59. Tafel, interview, December 12, 2001.

60. Lipman, p. 62.

61. "New Architecture Proves Practicability in Test Here," *The Racine Journal Times,* June 7, 1937.

62. Lipman, p. 65. Julie Sloane suggested in her book, *Light Screens: The Complete Leaded Glass Windows of Frank Lloyd Wright* (Rizzoli, 2001), that Wright reached back to traditional Japanese design in designing the glass tube clerestory windows. She wrote that the window tubes are evocative of "Bamboo Curtain," an illustration in Edward Sylvester Morse's *Japanese Homes and Their Surroundings,* Boston, 1886, a book that she thought Wright may likely have read early in his career.

63. Courtesy the McCormick Library of Special Collections at Northwestern University.

64. Meehan, p. 14.

65. *The Meyer May House,* Grand Rapids, Michigan, booklet for tour guests, Grand Rapids: Steelcase, 1987, p. 2.

66. Lipman, interview, February 5, 2002; magazine available at reference desk of the Racine Public Library.

67. "Between the Lines," *The Racine Journal Times,* April 24, 1939.

68. "Johnson Offices Open to Public, Presence of Royalty to Bring Housewarming to a Climax," *The Racine Journal Times*, April 21, 1939.

69. *The Racine Journal Times Sunday Bulletin,* April 23, 1939.

70. Ron Wolter, interview with the author, March 13, 2001.

71. Samuel C. Johnson, *The Essence of a Family Enterprise.* Racine: S. C. Johnson & Son, Inc., 1988, p. 137.

72. Johnson, interview with the author, August 27, 2001.

73. Tafel, interview, December 12, 2001.

74. Tafel, p. 185; $200,000 in 1936 is equivalent to $2.59 million in 2002; $750,000 in 1936 –1939 is equivalent to $9.7 million in

2002; and $5 million in publicity in 1939 is equivalent to $64.8 million in 2002. John J. McCusker, "Comparing the Purchasing Power of Money in the United States (or Colonies) from 1665–2002," Economic History Services, 2003, http://www.eh.net/hmit/ppowerusd/.

75. George Nelson, "Making Bridges," in Edgar Tafel, *Frank Lloyd Wright: Recollections by Those Who Knew Him.* New York: Dover, 1993, p. 228.

76. The letters and plans © 2004 Frank Lloyd Wright Foundation and used with permission of the Foundation and of the Research Library of The Getty Research Institute in Los Angeles. The note from Wright to Johnson on the floor plan was transcribed by OsKär Muñoz, Frank Lloyd Wright Foundation.

77. McCusker.

78. Lipman, p. 122.

79. Ibid., p. 37.

80. One of these letters, dated December 14, 1943, is republished as Appendix A in this book.

81. Lipman, p. 143.

82. Bruce Brooks Pfeiffer, *Frank Lloyd Wright Monograph* 1942–1950, edited and photographed by Yukio Futagawa. Tokyo: A.D.A. Edita, 1988 p. 44.

83. Wolter, interview with the author, July 13, 2001.

84. Robert McCarter, *Frank Lloyd Wright.* London: Phaidon Press, 1997, p. 196.

85. Lipman, p. 133.

86. Brendan Gill, *Many Masks: A Life of Frank Lloyd Wright.* New York: Putnam, 1987, p. 373.

87. Johnson, e-mail to the author, May 31, 2003.

88. Ibid.; Fred Billman, e-mail to the author, August 29, 2003; Lipman, p. 164.

89. Tom Casey, conversation with the author at Taliesin, May 28, 2003.

90. Johnson, interview, March 31, 2003.

91. Ibid., August 27, 2001.

92. Billman, interview with the author, May 30, 2003.

93. Johnson, August 27, 2001.

94. Ibid.

95. Ibid., August 27, 2001.

96. Lipman, p. 169.

97. Pfeiffer, floor plans and renderings, pp. 270–272.

98. Letters from January 30, 1950 and March 17, 1950, courtesy Racine Heritage Museum Collections; © 2004 The Frank Lloyd Wright Foundation.

99. Letters from the SC Johnson archives, reproduced with permission. © 2004 The Frank Lloyd Wright Foundation

100. Johnson, interview, March 31, 2003.

101. Bruce Brooks Pfeiffer, *Treasures of Taliesin: Seventy-Seven Unbuilt Designs of Frank Lloyd Wright.* San Francisco: Pomegranate, 1999, p. 106.

102. Christopher Paulson, executive director, Racine Heritage Museum, conversations with the author, 2002–2003.

Chapter 3

1. Robert McCarter, *Frank Lloyd Wright.* London: Phaidon Press, 1997, p. 231.

2. Quoted by McCarter, p. 271.

3. Wright's "Specifications" in the Monolith Homes Project Files, R. M. Schindler archive, Architecture and Design Collection, University Art

Museum at the University of California, Santa Barbara refer to "The Monolithic Home," but the project is commonly referred to as the "Monolith Homes."

4. Anthony Alofsin, *Frank Lloyd Wright: The Lost Years, 1910–1922.* Chicago: University of Chicago Press, 1993, p. 372, fn. 28.

5. Ibid.

6. Ibid.

7. Bruce Brooks Pfeiffer, archivist, Frank Lloyd Wright Foundation, e-mail to the author, April 12, 2003: ". . . the . . . drawings have been in our collections since 1919, and it was assumed that Wright was the architect. Only recently did we discover, through correspondence between Wright and Schindler, that it was indeed Schindler, although working in the office of Frank Lloyd Wright in Chicago."

8. Kathryn Smith, *Frank Lloyd Wright: Hollyhock House and Olive Hill.* New York: Rizzoli, 1992, p. 106, and Finis Farr, *Frank Lloyd Wright,* New York: Scribner's, 1961, p. 240.

9. Bruce Brooks Pfeiffer, *Frank Lloyd Wright Monograph 1914–1923,* vol. 5, edited and photographed by Yukio Futagawa. Tokyo: A.D.A. Edita, 1985, p.191.

10. Wright's "Specifications."

11. Pfeiffer, p.191.

12. Kathryn Smith, *Schindler House.* New York: Abrams, 2001, p. 14; Judith Sheine, *R. M. Schindler.* London, Phaidon Press, 2001, p. 51.

13. Smith, *Frank Lloyd Wright: Hollyhock House and Olive Hill,* p. 110.

14. Ibid.; Alofsin, p. 372, fn. 28.

15. Smith, *Frank Lloyd Wright: Hollyhock House and Olive Hill,* p. 110.

16. Ibid., chap. 11, fn. 4.

17. Jonathan Lipman, *Frank Lloyd Wright and the Johnson Wax Buildings.* New York: Rizzoli, 1986, p. 143; Sam Johnson, e-mail to the author, October 8, 2003.

18. Sam Johnson, e-mail, October 9, 2003.

19. Lipman, p. 143.

20. Johnson, e-mail, October 8, 2003.

21. Johnson, e-mail, October 9, 2003.

22. Lipman, e-mail, October 17, 2003.

AIA Journal, January 1979.

Alofsin, Anthony, *Frank Lloyd Wright: The Lost Years, 1910–1922.* Chicago: University of Chicago Press, 1993.

Alofsin, Anthony, ed., Introduction, *Frank Lloyd Wright: An Index to the Taliesin Correspondence,* 5 vols. New York and London: Garland Publishing, Inc., 1988.

The Architectural Forum, January 1938.

Buenker, John and Richard Ammann, *Invention City: The Sesquicentennial History of Racine.* Racine, WI.: Racine Heritage Museum, 1998.

Canine, Craig, *Wingspread.* Racine: The Johnson Foundation, Inc., 1997.

Carter, Brian, *Johnson Wax Administration Building and Research Tower.* London, Phaidon Press, 1998.

Farr, Finis, *Frank Lloyd Wright.* New York: Scribner's, 1961.

Gill, Brendan, *Many Masks: A Life of Frank Lloyd Wright.* New York: Putnam, 1987

Hanks, David A., *The Decorative Designs of Frank Lloyd Wright.* New York: Dutton, 1979.

Heinz, Thomas A., *The Vision of Frank Lloyd Wright.* Edison, NJ: Chartwell Books, 2000.

Henning, Randolph C., *At Taliesin: Newspaper Columns from Frank Lloyd Wright and the Taliesin Fellowship, 1934–1937.* Carbondale and Edwardsville, IL.: Southern Illinois University Press, 1992.

Hitchcock, Henry-Russell, *In the Nature of Materials: The Buildings of Frank Lloyd Wright 1887–1941.* New York: Duell, Sloan and Pearce, 1942.

Hoffmann, Donald, *Frank Lloyd Wright: Architecture and Nature.* New York: Dover, 1986.

Jacobs, Herbert, *Frank Lloyd Wright: America's Greatest Architect.* New York: Harcourt, Brace & World, 1965.

Johnson, Samuel C., *The Essence of a Family Enterprise.* Racine: S. C. Johnson & Son, Inc., 1988.

The Journal Times, *Celebrate Racine: A Look at a Unique Community,* 1997.

Karr, Susan E., *Architectural and Historical Survey of the City of Racine.* Racine: Racine Landmarks Preservation Commission, 1980.

Kinch, Richard, *Wingspread: The Building.* Racine: The Johnson Foundation, Inc., 1981.

Levine, Neil, *The Architecture of Frank Lloyd Wright.* Princeton, NJ: Princeton University Press, 1996.

Lipman, Jonathan, *Frank Lloyd Wright and the Johnson Wax Buildings.* New York: Rizzoli, 1986.

Macaulay, Stewart, *Organic Transactions: Contract, Frank Lloyd Wright and the Johnson Building.* Madison: *Wisconsin Law Review,* vol. 1996, no. 1.

Maddex, Diane, *Frank Lloyd Wright's House Beautiful.* New York: Hearst Books, 2000.

McCarter, Robert, *Frank Lloyd Wright.* London: Phaidon Press, 1997.

Meehan, Patrick J., *The Master Architect: Conversations with Frank Lloyd Wright.* New York: Wiley, 1984.

Museum of Modern Art, *Twentieth Century Engineering Exhibit Catalog.* New York: 1964.

Pfeiffer, Bruce Brooks, *Frank Lloyd Wright Monograph,* 12 vols., edited and photographed by Yukio Futagawa. Tokyo: A.D.A. Edita, 1984–1988.

Pfeiffer, Bruce Brooks, *Frank Lloyd Wright,* Cologne: Taschen, 2003.

Pfeiffer, Bruce Brooks, *Treasures of Taliesin: Seventy-Seven Unbuilt Designs of Frank Lloyd Wright.* San Francisco: Pomegranate, 1999.

Prairie Architects, *Wingspread Historical Structures Report.* Fairfield, IA: Prairie Architects, Inc., 1995.

Riley, Terrence, *Frank Lloyd Wright Architect.* New York: The Museum of Modern Art, 1994.

Rintz, Donald, *Frank Lloyd Wright and Prairie School Architecture: Tour Guide.* Racine: Racine Landmarks Preservation Commission, 1994.

Rintz, Donald, *Southside Historic District Walking Tour Guide.* Racine: Racine Landmarks Preservation Commission, 1993.

Secrest, Meryle, *Frank Lloyd Wright: A Biography.* New York: Knopf, 1992.

Sheine, Judith, *R. M. Schindler.* London, Phaidon Press, 2001.

Sloane, Julie L, *Light Screens: The Complete Leaded Glass Windows of Frank Lloyd Wright.* New York: Rizzoli, 2001.

Smith , Elizabeth A. T. and Michael Darling, *The Architecture of R. M. Schindler.* New York: Abrams, 2001.

Smith, Kathryn, *Frank Lloyd Wright: Hollyhock House and Olive Hill.* New York: Rizzoli, 1992.

Smith, Kathryn, *Schindler House.* New York: Abrams, 2001.

Sommer, Robin Langley: *Frank Lloyd Wright: A Gatefold Portfolio.* New York: Barnes & Noble,1997.

Storrer, William Allin, *The Architecture of Frank Lloyd Wright: A Complete Catalog.* Chicago: The University of Chicago Press, 2002.

Tafel, Edgar: *Years with Frank Lloyd Wright.* New York: Dover, 1979.

Tafel, Edgar, *Frank Lloyd Wright: Recollections by Those Who Knew Him.* New York: Dover, 1993.

Taliesin Preservation, Inc., *The Love of an Idea,* fund-raising brochure. Spring Green, WI: Taliesin Preservation, 1999.

Thomson, Iain, *Frank Lloyd Wright: A Visual Encyclopedia.* London: PRC Publishing, 1999.

Twombly, Robert C., *Frank Lloyd Wright: His Life and His Architecture.* New York: Wiley, 1979.

Wright, Frank Lloyd, *An Autobiography: Frank Lloyd Wright.* New York: Longmans, 1932.

Wright, Frank Lloyd, *An Autobiography: Frank Lloyd Wright.* New York: Horizon Press, 1977.

Wright, Frank Lloyd, *The Story of the Tower: The Tree That Escaped the Crowded Forest.* New York: Horizon Press, 1956.

Wright, Olgivanna Lloyd: *Frank Lloyd Wright: His Life, His Work, His Words.* New York: Horizon Press, 1966.

■   ■   ■